YORUBA WARFARE IN THE
NINETEENTH CENTURY

YORUBA WARFARE
IN THE NINETEENTH
CENTURY

BY

J. F. ADE AJAYI

*Professor in the Department of History, University of Ibadan, and
Sometime Senior Research Fellow of the
Institute of African Studies, Ibadan*

AND

ROBERT SMITH

Lecturer in History, University of Ife

CAMBRIDGE
AT THE UNIVERSITY PRESS
IN ASSOCIATION WITH THE
INSTITUTE OF AFRICAN STUDIES
UNIVERSITY OF IBADAN

1964

PUBLISHED BY
THE SYNDICS OF THE CAMBRIDGE UNIVERSITY PRESS

Bentley House, 200 Euston Road, London, N.W.1
American Branch: 32 East 57th Street, New York 22, N.Y.
West African Office: P.O. Box 33, Ibadan, Nigeria

©

CAMBRIDGE UNIVERSITY PRESS

1964

Printed by The Broadwater Press Limited
Welwyn Garden City, Hertfordshire

FOREWORD

by DR K. ONWUKA DIKÉ

Vice-Chancellor, University of Ibadan and
Director of the Institute of African Studies

Yoruba Warfare in the Nineteenth Century is the first book to be
published by the Institute of African Studies of the University
of Ibadan in association with Cambridge University Press. It
comprises a detailed account of the Ijaye war of 1860–5 by
J. F. Ade Ajayi, Professor in the Department of History of the
University and sometime Senior Research Fellow of the Institute of African Studies, and a general study of Yoruba Warfare
by Robert Smith, Lecturer in History at the University of Ife.
Though the two studies are happily complementary, they
were in fact written independently and it was only by coinci-
dence that they were read together at the Congress of the
Nigerian Historical Society, of December 1962. At that time
the Institute had already committed itself to publishing Professor Ajayi's study as a monograph, but since Mr. Smith had
reached similar conclusions about the wars in his own more
general study, it was felt that a more valuable book would
result if the two were published together.

There is little need to stress to the student of African history
the importance of the Yoruba people. They number many
million, and are to be found not only in their homeland of
Western Nigeria but throughout West Africa and as far afield
as Brazil and Cuba, where their culture still exerts a strong
influence. This culture has produced some of the world's
masterpieces in sculpture, notably the bronzes and terra cottas
of Ife, and has also strongly influenced the art of Benin.

I would like to make a few points about the importance of
this particular study. Too often the Yoruba wars—indeed
most African wars—which lasted for the best part of the nineteenth century, have been described as extended slave raiding
or as mere internecine conflicts. These were rationalizations
which Europeans later used as *post facto* justifications for

their occupation of tropical Africa. They had come, it was often claimed, to confer 'peace and civilization' in place of chaos and disorder. But this study, I believe, amply demonstrates the complicated political social and economic changes that this part of West Africa was undergoing at the time, and of which these wars were but a reflection. The study of the dramatic collapse of the Oyo Kingdom in the face of these forces is essential to an understanding of nineteenth-century Nigerian history, especially in so far as it concerns European penetration of the interior and the southward expansion of the Fulani Empire.

These two studies give us a valuable insight into the interaction of war and politics in pre-colonial Africa, and indicate that detailed study of aspects of African history in the nineteenth century is possible by a judicious use of documentary and oral evidence as well as material artefacts. I am pleased that the authors decided to include Captain Jones's *Report on the Egba Army in 1861* which will be most useful to students of African history as an example, whatever its prejudices, of how Europeans involved in these wars viewed Yoruba military organization. This book has greatly enhanced my own understanding of an important aspect of nineteenth-century Nigerian history.

CONTENTS

MAPS AND PLANS

ix

ABBREVIATIONS

In the notes the author's name only is given; official papers are referred to by the abbreviations listed below. Full details of all references are given in the bibliography.

C.M.G. *Church Missionary Gleaner*

C.M.I. *Church Missionary Intelligencer*

C.M.P. *Church Missionary Proceedings*

C.M.S. Church Missionary Society, London

M.M.S. Methodist Missionary Society, London

P.P. Parliamentary Papers

P.R.O. Public Record Office, London

S.B.C. Southern Baptist Convention, Richmond, Virginia, U.S.A.

S.M.A. Société des Missions Africaines, Rome

INTRODUCTION

A Historical Note on the Yoruba People

For the Yoruba people of Western Nigeria, history began at Ile-Ife in the heart of the evergreen forest. The town is regarded as the cradle of the Yoruba culture. One tradition says that it was at Ile-Ife that man was created. Another says that when Oduduwa, the mythical ancestor, arrived from far away in the east, Ile-Ife was the place where he settled and that it was from there that his children and grandchildren went to found the various ruling dynasties among the Yoruba and neighbouring peoples. His eldest daughter, it is said, was the mother of the Olowu of Owu; another was the mother of the Alaketu of Ketu. One son became the Oba of Benin, another the Alake of Ake (now part of Abeokuta), another the Onisabe of Sabe, another the Alafin of Oyo. Others became the Awujale of Ijebu-Ode, the Osemawe of Ondo, the Ore of Ottun, the Ewi of Ado-Ekiti, the Elekole of Ikole, and so on.

That is to say, the traditional culture of the Yoruba people is associated with the town of Ile-Ife: it was there that they first became conscious of themselves. From a nameless people wandering around with crude and simple stone and iron tools, they evolved a common language, a monarchical system of government, an urban social life, a pattern of religious beliefs and practices and a famous artistic tradition. Thus Ile-Ife represents the formative stage in the cultural development of the Yoruba people. Most of the traditional *orisas* or deities, as distinct from the imported ones, are said to have originated there. All the important traditional rulers who have the right to wear beaded crowns trace their origin there, and many of them used to send to Ile-Ife for sacred symbols to use at their coronations.

The Yoruba people have a common language and a common culture but they did not evolve a common political state. It is doubtful whether they even had a common name for

B   I

themselves. Some of their neighbours called them *Olukumi*, probably as a nickname, and referred to their language as *Anago*. It was in the process of searching for a standard Yoruba to reduce to writing that the missionaries began to extend the name Yoruba (Yoöba), the language of the Oyo section, to cover all the Anago-speaking peoples. The various cities and kingdoms that were founded developed separately, each according to the resources of the area where they were situated and the ability of their rulers to use those resources, subject always to the changes and chances of history. Some became large and powerful, others became small and insignificant. The kingdoms of Benin founded among the Edo, outside the Yoruba country, became very powerful along the coast. Of the other kingdoms regarded by tradition as most important in the early days, Owu is now a little quarter in Abeokuta; Ketu and Sabe are little more than small towns in Dahomey; Illa is no longer as large or as important as tradition would have us believe. Each of these cities and kingdoms has its own history, its own dialect and cultural variations.

By the beginning of the nineteenth century, the different kingdoms could be grouped into a number of sub-cultural divisions: Oyo, Egba, Egbado, Ijesha, Ife, Ijebu, Ekiti, Ondo, Akoko. In some of these divisions, like Oyo, one single ruler was paramount. In others, like Ijebu, single rulers were in the ascendancy, but their paramountcy was not yet generally acceptable. In other areas, notably Ekiti, there was an accepted plurality of crowned rulers and none was paramount. Of these divisions, Oyo was the largest and most populous; and because of his clear ascendancy throughout Oyo, the Alafin was the most powerful Yoruba ruler, and the Oyo empire came nearest to bringing all the Yoruba people under one political influence.

Tradition says that Oyo was founded by Oduduwa's youngest son, Oranyan. Some even say Oranyan was his grandson. What seems certain is that Oyo was one of the latest Yoruba kingdoms to be founded, and to start with, one of the most junior: but it soon became the most important. The

BALOGUN IBIKUNLE'S RITUAL STOOL: now in the possession of Chief
J. A. Ayorinde, Ministry of Agriculture, Ibadan. Chief Ibikunle was the
Commander-in-chief of the Ibadan forces in the Ijaye War. It is said that
he used this stool whenever he consulted the oracle, or attended other
important religious ceremonies, or when in council or in war he wished to
make crucial decisions.

The decoration on the cover is based on a detail from this carving and
shows a warrior and his captive slave.

Facing p. 2

capital of this kingdom was not the present Oyo, 30 miles from Ibadan, but the place marked Old Oyo on the map, on the border of the Western and the Northern Regions. Whereas Ile-Ife and many other Yoruba towns were situated in the thick evergreen forest, Old Oyo was sited in the savannah belt close to the Niger.

Oyo owed its rise to power to its position. The soil around it was fertile, and farming was its most important occupation. But apart from farming, Old Oyo became the leading trading centre south of the Niger. In the first place, Oyo traded with all parts of the Yoruba country. There were well-known trade routes connecting it with all the most important markets of those days. The routes were guarded. Traders gathered at agreed times and places and travelled together in caravans. In this way, Oyo became an important centre for gathering the produce of the rain forests to sell to people of the drier savannahs. In addition, Oyo had the best weavers and some remarkable blacksmiths whose products were in great demand. Oyo traded not only across the Niger to Kano where they met traders from the far north of Africa, they were probably also in touch with places like Gao, Timbuctoo, and Jenne on the Niger. From this distant trade, Oyo imported such articles as salt, leather goods, antimony and glass ware. But the most significant imports were horses which formed the basis of the political power of Old Oyo.

Before horses were introduced, Oyo was a small kingdom struggling with Borgu and Nupe for a foothold in that very strategic centre near the Niger. Then, probably about the middle of the sixteenth century, Nupe conquered Oyo. The Alafin and his chiefs at first took refuge in Borgu. Then they built a new capital temporarily at Igboho. It was at this time that the Oyo began seriously to think of improving their army and making it as powerful as those of their northern neighbours by using horses and training soldiers who could fight on them. Perhaps there were already a few horses in Oyo before then. But it was Alafin Orompoto of this period whom we first hear of using horsemen in a large way. Tradition says he had a thousand horsemen, and he used to tie leaves to the horses' tails so that when they went to fight, the leaves swept the ground after them to cover up their trail. With this cavalry, Oyo quickly became more powerful than both Borgu and Nupe. Within the next hundred years or so, Old Oyo was rebuilt, the Alafin became dominant among the Oyo, and the Oyo people began to create an empire. They conquered Sabe and Ketu, and expanded down both sides of the river Ogun to the coast. Through Porto Novo, which they called Ajase, they traded with the Europeans. A European trader towards the end of the seventeenth century wrote that the coastal people feared Oyo horsemen so much that the very mention of their name made them tremble. With this cavalry force, Oyo maintained in the seventeenth and eighteenth centuries the most powerful political state in the Yoruba country.

The empire was in three parts. First, was the metropolitan area consisting of those who spoke 'Yoöba', the Oyo dialect, and who owed direct allegiance to the Alafin. They were divided into six provinces, three to the west of the upper Ogun or right bank (Ekun Otun), and three to the east or left bank (Ekun Osi). Secondly, there were the other Yoruba people conquered or dominated by the Oyo-speaking ones. The most important of these were the Egba and Egbado on both sides of the Ogun, south of the metropolitan provinces. Thirdly, there were the non-Yoruba people who were not directly controlled but were forced to pay tribute from time to time. Of these, Dahomey was controlled for longer periods than either Borgu or Nupe. What is important to notice is that because this empire was so dependent on its cavalry force, the Alafin never succeeded in bringing all the Yoruba into the empire. He was most powerful in the open savannahs where horses could move easily and the deadly tsetse fly was less rampant. He had little power in the forests and hills of Ekiti and Ondo, Ife and Ijebu. Rather than seek to conquer such difficult areas, Oyo expanded west towards Dahomey, and to the north in the Borgu and Nupe countries.

Nevertheless, in spite of these limitations, it would appear

4

that while the Old Oyo empire lasted, its power and prestige helped to prevent the incidence of major wars, not only within its frontiers, but also throughout the Yoruba country. This power and prestige was available to settle crises which could not be resolved by reference to the common origin of the Yoruba Obas and their traditional positions in the hierarchy of the Yoruba 'family'. The decline of the empire at the end of the eighteenth century, and its collapse early in the nineteenth, precipitated the wars which are the subjects of the following essays. The first essay deals with the general character and techniques of the wars. The second makes a detailed study of one of them. In the appendix there is an eye-witness account of the same war by a British military officer, published for the first time.

PART I

THE YORUBA WARS
c. 1820–1893

ACKNOWLEDGEMENTS

The writer expresses his gratitude to his many helpers in Nigeria, especially: the Ataoja of Oshogbo, the Oloffa of Offa and his chiefs, the Olukuku of Okuku and his chiefs, the Akirun of Ikirun, the Jagun and other chiefs of Ikirun, the Olu of Inisha and his chiefs, the Egburu of Iba, the Bale of Ijaye and his chiefs, the Bale of Olokemeji, the Bale Adepoju, the Bale of Iwawun, Mr. Akanni Akinlawon of Abeokuta, the authorities at the University of Ibadan (for use of the library), and his colleagues and students of the University of Ife.

The passage on the battle of Oshogbo is extracted from an article by the writer in *The African Historian*, the periodical of the undergraduate Historical Society at the University of Ife, by kind permission of the editors.

I

A CENTURY OF WARFARE

During almost the whole of the nineteenth century the country of the Yoruba was beset by warfare. It was the scene of a fratricidal war which lasted over 70 years, and of invasions from the north by the Fulani who early in the century established a base at Ilorin, south of the Niger and in Yorubaland itself, and from the west by the Dahomi. As elsewhere, war was progenitor and accelerator of change. The power of Oyo, the Yoruba's ancient metropolis, was challenged and then superseded by states which either had arisen during the preceding centuries, like Ijebu, or grew out of the unsettled conditions of the times, like Ibadan. The wars increased the supply of slaves for the still-expanding market and hindered the development of 'legitimate' trade in palm-oil. The military picture is less clear. The most important development was the steady advance in the use of firearms, but much of the evidence about the nature of the fighting and the conduct of the operations is contradictory. On the one hand there are the disparaging references to Yoruba morale and military prowess by Anglo-Saxon travellers such as the Landers and Burton.[1] On the other hand there are accounts (preserved by Johnson, the Oyo historian[2]) of epic conflicts resulting in numerous casualties, and stirring descriptions by missionary witnesses of engagements at, in particular, Abeokuta and Ijaye.[3] There

---

[1] Lander, pp. 134–5, 142–3, describes the supineness of the Oyo administration of 1830 in the face of the Fulani threat. The people, under the rule of 'the pusillanimous Mansolah' [Alafin Majotu] had 'neither foresight, nor wisdom, nor resolution, to put themselves in a posture of defence'. See also Burton, passim.

[2] Johnson, passim.

[3] For the defence of Abeokuta against the Dahomi in 1851, see *C.M.I.*, 1851, pp. 165–6; and Bowen, ch. xii. For the Ijaye war, see *C.M.P.*, 1860–1, pp. 50–2, and 1861–2, pp. 45–7; and Stone, chs xviii–xx.

also exists a report made at mid-century by a Captain Jones of the West India Regiment on the capabilities of the Egba army;[1] this professional and dispassionate account, although limited in its scope, goes some way towards reconciling the divergencies.

Information about the military history of the Yoruba before the nineteenth century is scanty. But in the early sixteenth century the Oyo state seems to have been accounted a powerful rival to Benin, and a hundred years later was asserting its influence over most of the Yoruba peoples to the south. The Dutch merchant Bosman, in an apparent reference to an attack on Allada by the Oyo in 1698, wrote that the Yoruba army was 'all Horses' and that 'This Nation strikes Terror into all the circumjacent *Negroes*'. In the eighteenth century Norris described the Oyo as 'a great and warlike people' who from 1738 to 1747 had been raiding into Dahomey until the king there promised to pay them tribute, while at the turn of the century Adams wrote that the ruler of Oyo was said by the Allada people to have 'an organized army amounting to 100,000 men, composed of infantry and cavalry', a report which he treated sceptically; he had also heard that a French officer from a slave-ship had visited the capital and thought the army to be 'a tolerably efficient one'.[2] According to Oyo tradition, the Alafin sent out his army every second year, partly for spoils and partly as a military exercise. The Are-Ona-Kakanfo, senior general of the kingdom and head of the Esho, the Alafin's Noble Guard, was required by his office 'to go to war once in three years to whatever place the king named, and, dead or alive, to return home a victor or be brought home a corpse within three months'. Thereafter the army was disbanded and its chiefs and soldiers returned to their farms.[3] These conditions probably persisted from generation to generation until the emergence of rival states, the in-

[1] See Appendix.
[2] Bosman (1907), Letter xx, pp. 397–8. For the other references see Hodgkin, pp. 94, 167–9, 171–2.
[3] Johnson, pp. 75, 131.

troduction of firearms, and the general endemic warfare of the nineteenth century changed the pattern.

These wars in the nineteenth century can conveniently be divided into three periods: from about 1820 to about 1837, from about 1837 to 1878, and from 1878 to 1893.[1] The first period, that of the collapse and supersession of Oyo, opens with the outbreak in about 1820 of the Owu war, the first of the civil wars. This was soon followed by the revolt at Ilorin against the Alafin by Afonja, his Kakanfo, which gave the Fulani their foothold in Yorubaland, the overthrow of Oyo by the Fulani, and then the southward move of the Oyo people into the forests.[2] The period closes with the building by the emigrants of new towns, notably Ibadan (*c.* 1829) and Abeokuta (*c.* 1830), the enlargement of older towns like Ijaye, and the founding of a new capital in the south at Ago-Oja, renamed Oyo (*c.* 1837). In the second period the dominant issue was the struggle between the successor states to Oyo, and above all between Ibadan and Abeokuta; the Ijaye war of 1860–2 was soon transformed from a contest between the Ibadan and their kinsmen the Ijaye into one between Ibadan and the Ijaye's allies, the Egba of Abeokuta. By this time the Fulani menace had lessened, after their defeat by the Ibadan at Oshogbo in *c.* 1840; henceforth the role of the Ilorin was virtually confined to intervention on one side or other (but always against Ibadan) in the civil wars and there seems no indication of any 'fifth column' in their favour among the Moslem traders who were now penetrating southern Yorubaland. On the other hand the invasions of the Dahomi had begun, with their fierce onslaughts on Abeokuta in 1851 and 1864, their attempts to create and lead an anti-Egba coalition among the Yoruba, and their later raids which lasted almost to the occupation of Dahomey by the French in the early 1890's and

[1] Johnson describes some 50 separate wars or campaigns between *c.* 1817 and 1893.

[2] A. I. Akinjogbin, in a personal communication, has suggested the following chronology for the opening stages of the Yoruba wars: 1821, the outbreak of the Owu war; 1824, the revolt of Afonja; 1827, the fall of Owu. The dating of Afonja's revolt is based on references in Clapperton, pp. 25, 28.

resulted in the loss of the western Yoruba kingdom of Ketu. The period also saw the first intervention in the wars by the British when in 1865 a company of the West India Regiment was despatched by Glover, the Lieutenant-Governor of the new colony of Lagos, to drive off the Egba from the siege of Ikorodu. This action was prompted by the injury to Lagos trade caused by the Egba's attempts to place tolls on the roads to the interior and to deny alternative routes to the traders. The last phase, that of the Ekiti wars, centred around a general coalition against the Ibadan who had emerged from the second period as the greatest power in the country. The coalition was headed by the Ekiti, a people who seem never to have acknowledged the suzerainty of Oyo and who now allied themselves with the Ilorin as well as with most of the other Yoruba states. The war was fought both in the north around Ikirun, where the Ibadan won an important victory in 1878, and Kiriji (onomatopœically named from the report of the rifles), and in the south where Ibadan faced the Egba and Ijebu. From 1886 peace negotiations were in train, mainly as a result of the efforts of the Governor at Lagos,[1] but not until the decisive defeat in 1892 of the Ijebu by a force from Lagos using modern weapons (including a Maxim and a seven-pounder as well as the demoralizing rockets)[2] was it possible to impose peace on all the contestants. On his famous trek in 1893 Governor Carter persuaded the Ibadan and Ilorin armies to break up their war-camps and return to their towns, and the series of treaties was signed which established the British Protectorate over what was to be Western Nigeria.

---

[1] From the establishment of British rule in Lagos, the administration there took a lively interest in the possibility of bringing about a peace. In 1861 the Acting Consul, McCoskry, wrote to the Foreign Office that 'any war in the Yoruba country vitally affects the trade of Lagos and if peace could by any means be maintained between its various tribes the development of the resources of the Country would be great and speedy' (P.R.O., Lagos despatch no. 4, 31 May 1861).

[2] Rockets had been effectively used by the British against Porto Novo in 1861, after which Consul Foote wrote, 'we can do anything we like now with the chiefs. They are terrified beyond belief. The rockets are called fearful war fetiches' (P.R.O., Foote to F.O., 9 May 1861 and 10 May 1861). They were used again at Ikorodu in 1865, occasioning more fear than casualties.

II

THE ARMIES AND THEIR WEAPONS

In considering the means by which these protracted wars were waged by the Yoruba, Johnson's account of their military organization is a valuable starting point.[1] It is true that this is confined to a description of the army of the Alafin of Oyo, but it seems that, rather as the political organization of Oyo was repeated with modifications in many of the other kingdoms, so did its army provide the pattern for other Yoruba armies in which the same titles and functions, and the same groupings by age, rank and experience occur.[2] Again, Johnson's detailed description of the Oyo army in its heyday may seem, especially to a reader acquainted with the strictures of Lander and Burton, so schematic as to be misleading. Nevertheless this dichotomy between the actual and the ideal (or 'establishment') is a commonplace in any army, and especially in one on active service.

As Johnson writes, there was no standing Yoruba army. The Yoruba host (rather like that of England in the days of 'bastard feudalism') was composed essentially of a number of important leaders and their followers, each chief bringing with him his personal armed retainers and also a much larger group bound to him by family or other allegiance and called from their peacetime occupations on the proclamation of war. Many chiefs, especially at Ibadan, also brought with their

[1] Johnson, pp. 131–7.
[2] Forde, pp. 19–22. Forde, quoting an unpublished thesis by Fadipe, writes that there are four main patterns of government among the Yoruba: (i) the Oyo chiefdoms, (ii) the Ife, Ijesha and Ekiti chiefdoms, the first being the model for the rest, (iii) the Ijebu chiefdoms, modelled on that of Ijebu-Ode, and (iv) the Egba and Lagos states. He adds: 'There were basic similarities among all varieties and also among the different Bale-ships.' The organization and operation of the armies were probably less dissimilar than those of the governments.

contingents household slaves trained for war, these constitut-
ing the nearest approach to regular troops among the Yoruba.
At Ibadan the various subordinate towns were required to
make contributions to the main army; Igangan, for example,
some 50 miles to the north-west, was bound in war to send a
quota of armed men, food and ammunition.[1] Burton described the Egba army as consisting of the chiefs with their followers and at their heels a 'mob of sutlers' carrying on their
heads the arms, ammunition, beds and provisions of the fighting men.[2] Certainly the impression created by the Yoruba
armies on the move—as by most other armies—must have
been a confusing one. But Johnson's analysis, borne out by
Jones's expert observation, gives coherence to the picture.
Each chief bore a senior or junior war title, and this indicated
broadly the nature of his command and the place of himself
and his followers in battle. These chiefs were the Oyo Ile, or
bearers of titles conferred by the ruler of a town.[3] At the centre
of the army was the Balogun or commander-in-chief, with a
series of subordinates: the Otun, commanding the right wing,
the Osi, commanding the left wing, the Asipa, their equal, and
after him in order the Ekerin, Ekarun and Ekefa. The younger
chiefs and their followers, on whom the brunt of battle generally fell, were grouped separately under the Seriki, while the
van was commanded by the Asaju, and the cavalry by the
Sarumi. Each of these generals had lieutenants bearing similar titles to those of the Balogun's veterans and exercising similar commands. Finally, a number of older chiefs representing
the king (who himself rarely took the field)[4] accompanied the
army as advisers and guardians of the camp and baggage train.
These arrangements, simple, flexible and time-honoured,
seem by and large to have been adhered to not only in the

---

[1] Forde, p. 39. [2] Burton (1863), Vol. I, p. 289. [3] Forde, p. 23.

[4] At the battle of Ilorin (c. 1835) Alafin Oluewu fought in the centre of the
army with his ally, Eleduwe, king of the Nikki. The Yoruba chiefs, with the
exception of those of Ibadan, deserted the king and the day was lost, Oluewu
being captured and put to death. This defeat was followed by the abandonment
of Old Oyo. After the accession of Alafin Atiba, who refounded Oyo, it was decided that the Alafin should no longer take the field in war. See Johnson,
pp. 263–8, 282, 287.

older monarchies among the Yoruba but also by the new republican power at Ibadan and the composite Egba state at Abeokuta.

Johnson's account of the Oyo army may be supplemented by Jones's description of the Abeokutan forces in 1861. Jones's report begins with an account of the constitutional steps required among the Egba before a state of war could be decided upon.[1] Since there was no regular army, a decision to make war was followed by the raising of troops. The Egba soldiers were 'almost without exception' farmers or other free civilians. Enlistment was nominally voluntary but usually pressure was put on the able-bodied; Jones heard that the Alake's government issued an edict before the Ijaye war that 'whosoever did not proceed at once to the war should be deprived of his heart'. Arming themselves according to their means, the troops would join their respective chiefs who, after paying contributions to the expenses of the war, moved with their followers to a rendezvous appointed by the Balogun. Jones compares the composition of the army in this way to the organization of a European army into brigades and regiments, but adds that the commander-in-chief remained 'altogether ignorant' of the numerical strength of his command.

The part played in battle in this century by the once-important Yoruba cavalry was small. At the beginning of the wars the Fulani derived considerable advantage from the mobility of their well-mounted horsemen; their victory in the Mugba-Mugba ('locust fruit') war, for example, was due to this superiority.[2] Among the Yoruba, only the chiefs and their personal retainers were by now regularly mounted, the latter being employed mainly in carrying messages and bringing up stragglers. Horses were otherwise little used by the Yoruba at this time, although there are references to mounted troops being present with the Egba army during the Ijaye war.[3] The Yoruba horses seem to have been of variable quality and the establishment of the Fulani in the north of the country had

---

[1] See Appendix.   [2] Johnson, p. 202.
[3] Stone, ch. XVIII; Burton (1863), Vol. I, pp. 292–3.

interrupted the supply of fresh stock;[1] nevertheless Jones noted that the Egba horses were 'numerous and hardy, requiring little attention and feeding on grass', so that 'a very excellent irregular cavalry might be speedily organized'. This inattention to the use of cavalry was illustrated at the battle of Oshogbo in which the Ibadan captured a large number of horses but used these mainly as food. But as the wars moved south into closely wooded and tsetse-ridden country, cavalry was becoming less useful and most actions seem to have been decided by the infantry with their firearms.

These foot-soldiers, writes Jones, were 'docile, obedient to command, capable of enduring great bodily fatigue and marching with ease 40 miles a day with loads on their heads'; once roused, they became 'fierce and bloodthirsty'. They were armed at the beginning of the century mainly with bows and arrows (some at least of the latter would have been dipped into poison) and swords, mostly of local manufacture; these swords were either the short *jomo* or the heavier *ogbo* or *agedengbe*. In 1861, of those few members of the Egba infantry who were without guns, some carried swords, which were 'always straight, double-edged, about three feet long', and wore pistols as a supplementary weapon, while there were, Jones observed, 'but very few spearmen and but an occasional bow and arrow'. The shield (*apata*) was apparently known but does not seem to have been a regular part of military equipment in this century. Clapperton, when riding to Old Oyo in 1826, was escorted by bowmen wearing 'natty little hats and feathers, with the jebus, or leathern pouch, hanging by their side'.[2] The Egba foot-soldiers in the 1860's wore distinctive *shokoto* (baggy trousers) and striped war jackets, and each carried slung from his right shoulder a leather bullet bag and a powder flask which was either a calabash or a skin.[3]

---

[1] Clapperton, pp. 34–5; Ajayi, pp. 42–3, quoted by Hodgkin, p. 46, note 3. The cavalry tradition of Oyo is a reminder that the original centre of the state, at Old Oyo, was well to the north of the forest.

[2] Clapperton, pp. 34–5.

[3] Jones (see Appendix); Burton (1863), Vol. I, pp. 292–3; *C.M.G.*, 1852, p. 115 (which contains a drawing of a Dahomian cartouche belt).

Just as the latter part of the nineteenth century saw European armies and warfare transformed by the introduction of rifled barrels, breech-loaders, cartridges, high explosive shells, and eventually automatic or quick-firing guns, so did the wars in Yorubaland at this time undergo a transformation caused by the spread of firearms. In West Africa the introduction of firearms was gradual, as it had been in Europe (where, as Bindoff writes, '. . . gunpowder was no atomic bomb revolutionizing warfare at a stroke').[1] Muskets had been brought to Benin by the Portuguese in the sixteenth century and, as part of their regular trade, by the Dutch in the 1690's.[2] Even earlier, firearms had crossed the Sahara into the Sudan, and the Mai Idris Alooma, who reigned in Bornu at the end of the sixteenth and in the early seventeenth century, had a body of Turkish musketeers in his army and household slaves expert in musketry.[3] Muskets had long been a staple of the barter trade in slaves on the coast; 'But for this the few thousands in the Delta could not have maintained their privileged position in the Atlantic trade and played the role of economic dictators to the millions in the hinterland', writes Dike.[4] Yet not until the 1820's did Yorubaland begin to be affected by the use of firearms. The first of the Yoruba to arm themselves in this way were the Ijebu who, as coastal people, were in touch with the white traders as were the Delta merchants. The earliest decisive use of firearms was probably in the Owu war (the first of the civil wars of the nineteenth century), when the fall of Owu after a long siege was attributed to the defenders' lack of guns.[5]

[1] Bindoff, S. T., *Tudor England*, London 1958, p. 52.

[2] Ryder, p. 251 and note.

[3] Ibn Fartua, *The Kanem Wars* quoted by Palmer, p. 22. Boahen writes that 'guns and ammunition were not exported from the north until the very last decade or two of the nineteenth century. . .' Barth found that muskets on sale in the Kano market in 1851 were imported via Nupe and at a review of troops in Katsina that among several hundred horsemen armed with straight swords and heavy spears only four or five muskets were to be seen. It seems likely that any medieval trade in firearms across the desert was on a small scale and had almost ceased by the beginning of the nineteenth century.

[4] Dike, p. 107.

[5] Johnson, pp. 207–10. An Owu chief, however, recently (June 1962) maintained that it was not the enemy's firearms but their greatly superior numbers which enabled them to starve the town into submission.

At Oshogbo in *c.* 1840 the Ibadan were still armed mainly with the long sword although a few had muskets. But by 1850 the musket had become the major weapon of the Yoruba armies and in 1851 Bowen noted that all the defenders of Abeokuta had guns. At Ikirun in 1878 both the Ibadan and their Yoruba enemies were almost all armed with short- and long-barrelled muskets (a few carried swords), while the Fulani cavalry fought with spears and bows.[1]

Until the introduction during the Ekiti wars of numerous American Sniders (breech-loading rifles), the best imported firearms were of Danish manufacture, which gave the name 'Dane gun' or 'Long Dane' to the muskets in general use. These were flintlock pieces, usually long-barrelled, costing in 1861 (according to Jones) 21*s.* 6*d.* They were fitted into stocks which were often of local manufacture and gaily painted, and were usually fired at arm's length or from the hip, owing to the violence of the recoil. A soldier would normally bring his own gun to war, but at least a part of the powder was provided for him. This powder was mostly imported from Boston, U.S.A., and was a coarse substance with a high charcoal content. Two hands' breadth was the usual charge (against three fingers' breadth in the old-fashioned Dane guns still used by many Yoruba hunters). The rate of fire can hardly have exceeded that of the matchlocks used in the English civil wars of the seventeenth century when one round was fired in three minutes, and the maximum range—disregarding accuracy—was between 200 and 400 yards; the effective range was at most 100 yards. The method of firing in the field, as described by Stone, the Baptist missionary at Ijaye, was that 'lines of men, several abreast, streamed to the front, fired and then turned and flowed back to the rear'.[2]

---

[1] The writer has in his possession a dilapidated gun which was bought in Ikirun and said to have been used in the Jalumi war. It is a flintlock, measuring 33 inches overall, with an unrifled barrel of 0·6 inches bore and 23 inches in length. The priming pan cover and frizzen are missing. The gun bears no visible marks of origin and may have been partly made and often reassembled locally. The flintlock mechanism, and the flint itself, are likely, however, to have been imported. (Brandon in East Anglia long supplied West Africa with flints.)

[2] Stone, ch. XVIII.

The ammunition consisted of bullets or bolts of bar-iron of varying sizes, cast and cut by local blacksmiths, who were also sword-makers. A number of the smaller sizes could be loaded and discharged at one time in order to produce a spray of fire which would somewhat counteract the inaccuracy of these smooth-bore weapons.

Artillery was little known even in the later stages of the Yoruba wars. Jones observed at Ijaye that each chief had 'a few pieces fired from rests with a bore of about $1\frac{1}{2}$ inches into which they put a handful of bullets and with these at close quarters they sometimes do great execution'. At Ijaye it is remembered that numerous palm trees there were damaged by gunfire during the war, and a proverb in Ibadan bears this out. The damage, which could hardly have been caused by muskets, was probably the work of these $1\frac{1}{2}$ inch pieces. At Abeokuta Jones was exercised over the indifference shown by the Egba to the seven guns (including a brass six-pound field piece) which had been presented to them by the British government at the insistence of the missionaries for their protection against the Dahomi. Despite the lessons in gunnery which the Abeokutans had received in November 1851 from Commander Forbes, R.N., who had been sent up from Lagos, the guns had been so neglected that they had become useless and were lying forlornly in various parts of the town, exposed to the climate and 'a roost for cocks and hens'. Burton told the 1865 Select Committee on Africa that he believed that the English howitzers had never taken the field; the Abeokutans did not understand their use and in any case considered that 'they eat too much powder'.[1]

The use of firearms influenced not only decisions on the battlefield but also, and perhaps to a greater extent, the political course of events; indeed the realization of the potentiality of fire-power seems to have preceded by many years its efficient application in action. The weapons and powder were all imported, and the struggle to ensure supplies was a factor of increasing importance. As in the Delta, control of

[1] PP, 1865, v (412), Q.2366.

the imports rested largely with the coastal peoples, but unlike
the Delta people, the people of the interior were generally
able to obtain supplies. The traders of Lagos and Ijebu
played a key part, while the lagoon-side town of Ikorodu was
the leading market. From the coast the arms usually travelled inland through Ijebu, and after the Ijebu monopoly had
been broken by the Egba, through Abeokuta, and an important element in Ibadan policy was to develop and protect
routes which should be independent of either of these two
trading powers.

Although many of the guns were of Danish origin and the
powder came mostly from the U.S.A., the British, as the protagonists of 'legitimate' trade, and after 1851 involved in the
affairs of Lagos, were deeply concerned in the arms traffic.
In 1851, stimulated by the missionaries, the British government authorized Beecroft, their consul for the Bights of Benin
and Biafra, to supply arms to the Egba, who were threatened
by the Dahomi, and to Badagry in order to protect that town
against the exiled King Kosoko of Lagos and to keep open the
road to Abeokuta.[1] Between July 1862 and the end of 1864
arms and powder worth some £23,000 were imported into
Lagos, most of it being transmitted to Ibadan through the
Ijebu middlemen at Ikorodu. This led to the Egba attack on
Ikorodu in 1865 and to the intervention there of the Lagos
government which was already concerned about the harmful
effects to the trade of their merchant community by Egba
attempts to control the roads to the interior.[2] Glover, the
Governor, imposed customs duties and then an embargo on
exports from Lagos to Abeokuta, the embargo being with-
drawn after protests from the missionaries at Abeokuta and
from some of the merchants. But as Newbury writes: 'The
defeat at Ikorodu was never forgotten; and it was well known
at Abeokuta that Glover had followed this up (as he told the
Colonial Office in 1866) by supplying large quantities of arms
to Ibadan and the Ijebu, while denying them to the Egba'.[3]

Not all these military imports were used for warfare. In-

---

[1] Biobaku, pp. 45–6.　　[2] Newbury, pp. 72–3.　　[3] *Ibid.* p. 90.

deed McCoskry, a Lagos merchant and Vice-Consul, told the 1865 Committee that the arms and powder were mostly used in firing salutes and that 'not one-tenth of the ammunition is expended in actual warfare'. This, as Burton later suggested to the Committee, was certainly an exaggeration.[1] As the wars continued, moreover, weapons and ammunition of an improved type were gradually replacing the flintlocks and locally manufactured bolts, with an increasingly important effect upon the military outcome. Soon after the Ijaye war the Egba succeeded in obtaining some breech-loading rifles and in 1881, during the Ekiti wars, a group of Ijesha living in Lagos sent a quantity of Snider rifles and cartridges to their kinsmen on the Kiriji battlefield. The Ibadan at Kiriji, who were already experiencing a severe shortage of ammunition, were dismayed by the casualties which these accurate, long-range and quick-firing weapons inflicted on them. They protested to their compatriots in Lagos, mentioning also the use against them of a Gatling machine-gun, but received no help. At length, however, they succeeded in obtaining from Ijebu traders some modern rifles and ammunition at high prices, paying £10 to £15 for a gun and sixpence for a cartridge; only thus were they able to maintain their position at Kiriji.[2]

Apart from the provision of firearms, ammunition and powder, commissariat problems were not serious for the Yoruba armies. They were operating among their own peoples and it was assumed that they would in case of need live off the land. 'Each fighting man from the Chief downwards feeds himself according to his own taste and fancies or needs', Jones observed, while Johnson writes that: 'By the rules of warfare *piye* or foraging was permitted', although in early times preserved food—parched beans and a special kind of hard bread made of beans and maize flour (*akara-kuru*)—had been taken

---

[1] PP, 1865, v (412), QQ. 1764–5 and 2386.

[2] Johnson, pp. 357, 452, 459–60, 490, 492. Only some 15 years before, the Prussians had demonstrated the superiority of their needle-gun at Sadowa, firing six shots to the Austrians' one, and in the war of 1870 the French made quite effective use of the Montigny machine gun (*mitrailleuse*)—their 'secret weapon'—as well as of the *Chassepot*.

into the field.[1] Most of the wars soon assumed a static character, and fields of maize and beans were planted by the attacking forces near their camps for later harvesting, while women came up to the rear to hold their markets. Jones noted that the prices asked at these markets for staple foods, such as cassava, provided an index to the state of supplies in the storehouses of the camp. Women also played a considerable role inside a besieged town, bringing to the wall the warriors' food and military supplies.

[1] Johnson, p. 132.

III

THE FORTIFICATION OF TOWNS AND CAMPS

Considerations of defence played an important part in Yoruba military policy. Probably the earliest settlements of the Yoruba, north of the forest, had generally been on such hill-top sites as those of the abandoned towns of Erin and Iwawun, some ten miles south south-west of Iseyin.[1] Many later towns, especially those founded after the onset of the Fulani *jihad*, were also sited with a view to repelling possible attack; this is strikingly illustrated at Ibadan which developed from a military camp occupying the summit and slopes of a range of hills, and at Abeokuta built among rocks and protected on the west by the river Ogun. Most towns in the south were situated within a belt of forest (the *Igbo Ile*) which was deliberately allowed to retain its thick undergrowth and was pierced only by narrow paths leading to the gates.[2] Every town of importance in the nineteenth century seems to have been surrounded by walls, almost always of earth, and ditches,[3] and in the older towns these must have been first constructed long—perhaps two or three hundred years—before the advent of the Fulani. The defences often consisted of both an inner wall, enclosing on a generous scale the built-up parts of the town, and an outer wall which protected farmland and supplementary sources of water as well as providing a first line of defence behind which the home army and its allies could form up before an attack (as they did at Oshogbo in *c.* 1840). The two walls were generally upwards of 100 yards apart and reflect a concept of defence in depth, preceding the use of firearms, which differentiates

---

[1] For the capture of Iwawun in 1861, see p. 42.
[2] Clapperton, ch. 1; Lander, p. 68; Stone, ch. v.
[3] Clapperton, ch. 1; *C.M.I.*, 1859, pp. 256–9.

23

them from the close double walls of cities and castles prevalent in both antiquity and the Middle Ages of Europe and the Near East. The capital at Old Oyo was surrounded by thick wood and an outer wall of some 15 miles' circumference; there were in addition at least one and possibly two inner walls with 'subsidiary extra walls in certain salients for strengthening of the defences' (Willett).[1] Ife, Owu, Ilesha, Ketu, Oshogbo, Ikirun and New Oyo are examples of towns protected by a double wall. At Erin the inner wall, or *odi Elerin*, encircling the citadel, was built exceptionally of large stones and is still in places about four feet high; the outer wall, below the hill, was entirely of earth and has now disappeared. At Abeokuta and Ibadan there was one main wall, although the growing population of the latter necessitated an extension by Balogun Ibikunle in 1858.[2] At Kishi, Lander noted that there was a double wall 'perforated with holes for bowmen to shoot through'.

The walls were of two types, either broad and high, or breastworks. At Old Oyo and Owu both the inner and outer walls are of the broad high type. The outer wall of the Ijebu kingdom (the *eredo*) is broad and high while the inner wall round the city of Ijebu-Ode seems to have been a breastwork. Well-preserved examples of these lower walls are at New Oyo, Oshogbo, Ikirun, Ijaye, and doubtless many other towns.[3] At New Oyo the distance between the inner and outer

---

[1] Clapperton, p. 58; Willett, p. 65. For the triple walls of Igboho, a town which for a time in the sixteenth to seventeenth centuries replaced Old Oyo as capital and which was taken and put to fire, probably by the Fulani after the fall of Oyo, see Lander, pp. 109–15 (second edition), and Clarke, pp. 87–8. Richard Lander estimated the circumference of the walls to be over 20 miles. Clarke, who saw the town some 20 years after it had been ruined and largely abandoned, wrote that the height from the bottom of the ditch to the top of the inner wall was between 15 and 20 feet.

[2] Johnson, p. 327. Bowen (p. 106) writes of Abeokuta: 'The walls, which include much open space, are probably fifteen miles in circuit, and the town itself is not less than ten miles in circuit.' See also the sketch map of Abeokuta and note on p. 145.

[3] At New Oyo the wall is known as the *odi amola* ('wall of our preservation'). At Ijaye the inner wall is known as the *odi agunrele* ('wall of our ascent homewards') and the outer wall on the west, said to have been built by the Egba army, as the *odi amonu* ('wall of our ruin'), probably in allusion to the disaster

walls (in places hardly 100 yards) is unusually small. The coronation shrine of Shango at Koso is situated between the two walls, and a separate but contiguous wall encircles the citadel-shrine of Igbo Shoro to the north-east.

It is difficult to deduce the strength of these walls from their remains today, which have been eroded by the fierce rains of many seasons and the operations of farmers (although their preservation has been helped by their being boundaries between farms of different ownership). There seems to have been a change in the character of the defence works early in the century, from predominantly broad-topped walls some 20 feet in height, and with correspondingly deep ditches, round the more important older towns such as Old Oyo and Owu, to lower less substantial walls or breastworks some five to eight feet high. It has been suggested that this development was due to the increasing use of firearms which could more conveniently be fired over this type of wall.[1] It may be urged against this attractive theory that whereas firearms do not seem to have come into general use until the period between 1840 and 1850, many towns were already provided with the lower wall in the 1820's and 1830's and possibly much earlier, but certainly towns of the importance of Ibadan and Abeokuta might be expected to have had walls on the greater scale had they been built a generation or more before. Walls of the second type were also built round the semi-permanent camps used in siege warfare. Freeman, the Wesleyan missionary who visited Abeokuta from Badagry in 1842, wrote that the Egba camp at Ado was 'surrounded by a mud-wall about five feet high and a ditch about four feet deep'.[2] Jones, describing the Egba camp at Ijaye, noted that the walls were sometimes given a sloping roof of thatch as a protection against the rain. He goes on

---

of 1862. Johnson (p. 91) claims that the terms *odi amola* and *odi amonu* are applied generally in Yorubaland to these outer walls.

[1] Omer-Cooper.

[2] Freeman, 3rd Journal, p. 216. See also *C.M.G.*, 1850–1, for extracts from Van Clooten's journal describing a visit to Ado in 1850. When the Egba abandoned their war camp, the Ado found themselves in possession of a flourishing farm inside its walls.

(rather in the manner of Tristram Shandy's uncle Toby) to criticize these defences, 'sufficient width is not given to the ditch, no slope is given to the scarp, the parapet is not sufficiently high, being seldom more than 4 or 5 feet high, without a *banquette*, its thickness is not sufficient being generally not more than 12–18 inches.'

The surrounding ditches were an important feature of the defences. They seem in places to have been dug on both sides of the wall (for example, at certain sections of the Ijaye and New Oyo walls), but usually are found only on the outside. They were of varying depth, depending on the height of the wall. Jones noted that the ditch was 'often extremely formidable, being much deeper in proportion than is usually admitted in systematic engineering'. Lander described the ditch at 'Assinara' in 1830 as being only 15 inches deep and three or four feet wide, 'so diminutive that a person might easily jump over it'. At Ketu, Owu, and almost certainly wherever the walls were of the older higher type, the ditches might be up to 15 or 20 feet deep and eight or nine feet wide.[1] Although in the wet season they temporarily assumed the character of a moat, they derived their main advantage as an obstacle to the enemy from the thorn bushes with which they were planted.

The ditches were crossed by bridges leading to the several town gates. As Lander saw at 'Assinara', a bridge might be a single plank serving as draw-bridge. At Old Oyo there were ten gates, at New Oyo only four, and at Ijaye five. Generally a customs house stood inside each gate for the exaction of tolls (on entering Ijaye in 1852, for example, Townsend, the Anglican missionary, paid 200 cowries on each load).[2] The gates were sometimes structures of considerable elaboration. The

[1] For a description of the fortifications at Ketu by Crowther, the Yoruba missionary, see the *C.M.I.*, 1853, p. 247. Crowther writes: 'There is a deep trench from fifteen to twenty feet deep around the town, with walls for fortification', and an outer ditch on the most exposed sector. He was much impressed by these defences which, he was told, had been built by a giant and which reminded him of 'the trenches around the Tower of London'.

[2] *C.M.I.*, 1853, p. 43. At New Oyo a house beside the inner wall is pointed out as being on the site of the Iseyin gatehouse and the senior inhabitant claims to be the grandson of the last gatekeeper.

Idena ('Sentry') gate at Ketu has inner and outer doors in deep porches, sited at an angle to each other and with the outer porch projecting across the line of the ditch. Between the porches is a courtyard with a covered verandah. The earthen walls are some two to five feet thick and the building is roofed with thatch which could be quickly removed in case of attack to prevent its being fired. (This gate, which is intact and in good repair, is probably the most important example of Yoruba military architecture in existence.) At Iperu, visited in 1855 by Dr Irving of the C.M.S., there were at least two thatched gates in the walls with inner and outer doors and flanking towers. These were in good repair, but a similar gate at Ofin was ruinous. At Ado, a few miles north-east of Badagry, visited in 1853 by Townsend and Crowther as peacemakers between the Ado and the Egba, the gate had two outer entrances across the ditch and an inner gate and wall. In addition to these fortified gates it was customary, at least among the Egba and Egbado, to place as watch-towers thatched huts raised on wooden stilts at intervals along the walls.[1]

Accounts of the Yoruba towns often refer, even at this stormy time, to neglect of the fabric of the walls.[2] In any crisis, however, the repair or rebuilding of a threatened sector would be an easy and speedy operation, as in 1851 at Abeokuta in the neighbourhood of the Aro gate. In a period of relative quiet, therefore, it was hardly necessary to expend time and labour on maintenance. But on going out to war the Yoruba armies found themselves required to turn to the task of constructing quite substantial new defences before engaging seriously with the enemy, since it was usual for them to form regular camps which both in their defences and the laying out of houses and

[1] Jones. For Irving's tour of Ijebu, see the *C.M.I.*, 1856, pp. 117–18. *C.M.I.*, 1853, pp. 275–8, contains a description of the visit by Townsend and Crowther to Ado. A plan of the main gate by Townsend illustrates the narrative and two engraved frontispieces (of drawings by Townsend) show the stilted and thatched watch-towers on the walls; in the drawings the gate and walls are hidden by high grass.

[2] Lander, p. 134 (Old Oyo, where the walls had been allowed to become 'a heap of dust and ruins'); Johnson, p. 314 (Abeokuta); Stone, p. 69 (Ijaye).

farms took on the appearance of settled towns. These camps were sited generally about an hour's march from the place to be attacked and on the banks of a stream. They were enclosed by a ditch and wall with watch-towers, apparently on the same plan as the permanent defences round many towns. The houses were built of mud or of bamboo and thatch, and arranged in separate areas for each chief and his followers. Jones observed that the Egba 'go to war in a very systematic manner as regards their present comforts'.

IV

THE STRATEGY AND TACTICS
OF THE WARS

The Yoruba wars were fought with only a limited regard for strategy. The breakdown in the authority of Oyo prevented the effective development of any policy which would protect the country from the Fulani and Dahomi invaders by reconciling the Yoruba states and co-ordinating their resistance. Yet after re-founding Oyo at Ago-Oja the Alafin Atiba attempted just such a measure. By conferring the title of Basorun[1] on Oluyole of Ibadan and of Are-Ona-Kakanfo (Generalissimo) on Kurunmi of Ijaye, Atiba hoped to mitigate the rivalry of these two leaders and their towns, and he laid down that in order to arrest the disintegration of the kingdom and to expel the invaders, Ibadan should have charge of the north and north-eastern defences and Ijaye of those to the west.[2] This plan, however, was soon defeated by the renewal of the civil wars—the Batedo war of 1844 between Ibadan and Ijaye, for example—and by the unwillingness of the other states to accept the leadership of either of the two palatinates designated by the Alafin.

As is usual in warfare, the direction of the Yoruba armies in the field reflected not only military exigencies but also the political preoccupations of the command and the personal relations between the commanders. Johnson's work again provides a starting point for the reconstruction of the theory according to which operations were conducted. He tells how the army, after sacrificing to the war standard, would move off

[1] The Basorun was the leading member of the Council of Seven at Oyo (the *Oyo Mesi*). He was entitled by his office to exercise a regency over the kingdom in the interim between the death of an Alafin and the installation of his successor.
[2] Johnson, p. 282.

29

in the order determined by the commands of the chiefs. In the front rode the Asaju, supported in his skirmishing by the mounted Bada, or knights. Next came the Seriki commanding the young warriors who would begin the real battle. The Balogun, accompanied by the senior chiefs and warriors, would observe, and in theory direct, the battle until the time came for him to intervene, while the horsemen would use their mobility to reconnoitre, cover retreats, cut off stragglers and try to demoralize the enemy by occasional sorties for prisoners. Johnson writes:

The usual method of a pitched battle, is for all the war chiefs to be disposed, each in his right place, according to their rank and title, or as the commander-in-chief disposes, and then each in turn to march forward, company by company to the middle line of battle to discharge their arms, trying each time to gain more ground. This method they call *tawusi*. But when later on the Balogun himself rises to fight, that denotes a general *charge* throughout the whole host; every man must be engaged in fight; and wherever he fixes his war standard, everyone is bound to dispose himself about it in due order. His going forward means that the whole army must push forward at whatever cost, for no one whose right place is in front dares fall to the rear of the Balogun except when *hors de combat*.[1]

Johnson describes the textbook manœuvre; the reality was naturally different. Jones's report on the fighting at Ijaye in 1861 provides a useful contrast. Battle was always preceded, Jones writes, by intensive intelligence activity, spies and bribery being much used. Once battle had been decided upon, it was 'a game of chance or deceit' for 'no general plan of attack or combination of movements is ever previously arranged'. The general took up his position well in the rear, usually near to a large tree suited for observation; most of the chiefs by this time had 'either reconnoitering glasses or telescopes with the use of which they are quite familiar'. When battle was joined, the action resolved itself into a series of isolated skirmishes. 'The movements of Brigades, Divisions in mass, hand to hand fighting, forcing of positions, and platoon firing' were 'alto-

[1] Johnson, pp. 134–7.

gether unknown', Jones alleges, although a reserve was usually kept. The troops 'spread themselves out anyhow into open order, and skirmish away until their ammunition is exhausted upon which they retire to replenish'. Jones continues:

Now herein consists one of the grand defects of their system. A. having, we will suppose, gained ground on his enemy B., the General never attempts to follow up and maintain his advantage by moving forward his reserve, but the whole army is kept at a standstill while the skirmish is going on in front. When A. retires therefore to replenish his ammunition the front of the battle is left in exactly the same position that it was at the commencement, and there it would continue throughout the day, did not the enemy B. usually at this period make an onward movement. Now the deceitful element comes into play, and a feigned retreat is not infrequently the result: this may or may not alter the fortunes of the day—if B. advances in force, it is possible that a very hard tussle may take place. Armed, however, with the musket, they avoid close quarters and form a habitual dislike to attacking walls. If A. makes a stand B. in his turn will retire and once more the tide of battle rolls back to the original point. Occasionally, if the ground is favourable, some attempt will be made to turn the flanks, but it often results in failure. Thus then proceeds the fight, a succession of advances and retreats, throughout the day, until sunset when, ammunition expended, begrimed and tired, each side draws off, victory being claimed according to the returns of killed and wounded, which usually is not large.

Jones's account was based on limited observation at a time when, as he admits, the Egba army had declined far from its standard of ten years before. Although objective and factual, it must not be accepted as giving the whole picture. Moreover, the ground observer of any battle must always be struck by its apparent confusion, and local conflict will seem to predominate. (The fictional battle scenes in Stendhal and Tolstoy are realistic because they reflect this point.) The implication that it was the use of the musket which accounted for the absence of close fighting is convincing, and for some years the new weapons must indeed have made war safer for the combatants. In the Gbanamu ('grasping fire') war, fought about 1830 by the Ibadan against the Ife and Ijebu, the Ibadan swordsmen

31

overcame their enemy by grasping and lifting their muskets by the barrels, thus rendering the fire harmless, but such tactics do not seem to have been repeated as firearms came into general use. Burton's view, derived from the more critical sections of Jones's report and from his own ironical observation at Abeokuta, far from the scene of war, is that these battles were always a kind of *champs de Mars* from which determination and tactics were generally absent and the weapons used absurdly ineffective. It may help to determine the extent to which this is so if four engagements, about three at least of which comparatively full and reliable information is available, are examined: these are the defeat of the Fulani of Ilorin at Oshogbo in about 1840, the successful repulse by Abeokuta of the Dahomi attack in 1851, the victory in a prolonged campaign of the Ibadan at Ijaye in 1861–2, and the victory of Ibadan over the Ilorin and their Yoruba allies at Ikirun in 1878.

V

A TURNING POINT: THE VICTORY
AT OSHOGBO, *c.* 1840

The battle of Oshogbo, which was fought in about 1840 and in which the Ibadan defeated the army of the Fulani from Ilorin, was probably the most important engagement of the long wars in nineteenth-century Yorubaland. Unlike some other notable battles where decision on the field affected little the subsequent situation—the defeat of the French by the Spanish Imperialists at Pavia in 1525, and in these wars the Ibadan victory at Ikirun in 1878 are examples—that at Oshogbo brought about profound military and political changes. The Fulani were decisively checked and Ibadan emerged as the leader among the states claiming to succeed to the power of Oyo. This then was one of those 'turning points' dear to historians. Yet comparatively little is known about the battle— even the year when it took place has not been determined with confidence[1]—since by the time that Johnson began to compile his *History of the Yorubas* many of the participants were dead and there had been no Christian missionaries at Oshogbo to record events as they were to do in later battles at Abeokuta and Ijaye. The present account attempts to combine Johnson's narrative, based on traditions about the battle preserved at Oyo and Ibadan,[2] with the traditions still current in Oshogbo itself.

By 1840 the impetus of the *jihad*, which had conquered the Hausa states and carried the Fulani east to Adamawa as well as south to Ilorin, had been largely spent, and a reverse at Gbodo about 1840 against a coalition of Yoruba and Borgu

---

[1] The usual date which is given in 1843, but this hardly accords with Johnson's narrative (pp. 289–97) of events between the battle and the Batedo war of 1844.

[2] Johnson, pp. 285–9.

forces had already shown that the *jihadis* were not invincible.[1]
Yet the ambition of the Fulani to extend their political empire
was still strong and the possession of Ilorin, within Yorubaland
itself, provided an excellent base for their further advance.
Meanwhile the Yoruba, after the fall of Oyo, had succeeded in
withdrawing southward towards the protective forests, founding new towns or enlarging old ones. Oshogbo was one of the
most northerly of these cities of refuge for the migrants—
Oshogbo ilu asala nigba isansa Oshogbo.[2] It lay on the edge of the
forest and was an important centre of the bush tracks connecting the towns of Yorubaland; six roads met here, from Ekiti,
Ilesha, Ife, Ibadan, Oyo and Ilorin. Its possession therefore
seemed necessary to the Fulani for the continuation of their
drive towards the sea. Like most Yoruba towns at this time it
was defended by a double mud-built wall (of the lower type,
about five feet high) and a ditch; the distance between the inner and outer wall was about half a mile. The diameter of the
outer wall was over three miles and the whole of the modern
town, except for the Trade School and Government College,
lies within the perimeter. The river Oshun to the south and
south-west provided a further defensive feature.

The Ilorin attack on Oshogbo—their third, according to
Johnson—was made by some 5,000 troops commanded by
Ali, the Hausa Balogun. The town was closely invested, and
the Oshogbo appealed for help to Ibadan which in the decade
since its foundation had grown from a war camp into a large
and important town. The Ibadan sent two contingents of their
soldiers to Oshogbo, but these proved unable to force the
Ilorin to lift the siege so that eventually the main army was
sent up under the command of the Balogun Odenlo (or Oderinlo). They entered Oshogbo from the south, crossing the Oshun

---

[1] Johnson, pp. 260–1, ascribes the successful raising of the seige of Gbodo (on
the upper Ogun) by the Ilorin to Borgu archery. In this battle, Atiba, the later
Alafin, fought as an ally of the Ilorin though on his orders his soldiers 'were
firing only gun-powder'. Chief O. S. Ojo, pp. 22–3, describes the battle as an
action by the warriors of Shaki in alliance with the Borgu.

[2] For accounts of the foundation of this town, see Olugunna; Johnson,
p. 156; and Beir, p. 97.

at the place now called Elegba in recollection of the 2,000 cowries paid by Odenlo to the ferrymen who transported his army.[1]

Some delay (20 days, Johnson says) ensued before the Ibadan were ready to launch a major attack on the Ilorin in their camp to the north-east of the town, towards Ikirun. The Ibadan were armed mainly with long swords (*agedemgbe*), but a few of their number carried muskets. The Ilorin carried spears and were mainly mounted, whereas among the Ibadan only the chiefs and their immediate entourage had horses. At last, at a council of war held at Idi Aka ('under the shade of the Aka tree') on the north-west side of the town,[2] it was decided to attack the Ilorin that evening as darkness fell, so as to offset the advantage to the enemy of their cavalry. The army formed up in the dusk between the inner and outer walls on the north-east, using as password the question and answer: 'What is the fare of the ferry? 2,000 cowries.' Then they passed beyond the outer wall at the place still known as Agbodogun, 'where the mortars (pounding the yams in the enemy camp) are heard', and fell on the Ilorin. They achieved what Professor Falls has called 'the most effective of all keys to victory', the surprise of their enemy. The Ilorin, caught sleeping in their tents,[3] were unable to mount any counter-attack and were soon in flight. Johnson describes graphically how the cavalry attempted to spur away their horses before remembering to untether them. The battle was a complete victory for the Ibadan and their allies. Many of the enemy were killed or taken captive, although the commander, Ali, succeeded in escaping with a group of followers. Skeletons of the horses slain by the Ibadan to prevent further escapes are said still to be found on the site of the battle.

[1] A bridge has lately been built here to connect Oshogbo with its farm settlement.

[2] The place of the war council is pointed out near to the railway crossing and station at the entrance to the town from Ede.

[3] The Ilorin, like other armies from the Sudan, apparently used tents in their war camps; the Yoruba usually preferred more permanent and comfortable quarters.

The result of the battle may be ascribed to several factors: first, the confusion of the Ilorin who had no expectation of a night attack—Oshogbo is an unusual and perhaps unique example of such tactics in the Yoruba wars—and then the inability of the Ilorin to use their cavalry in the darkness and in the fairly thickly wooded country which persists for a few miles north of Oshogbo. It is evident that the Ibadan derived little or no advantage from their firearms, but there is a third factor which seems to have been important: illness in the Ilorin camp among men and horses. The Oshogbo relate that their river goddess Oshun disguised herself as an old woman and sold poisoned yam flour (*amala*) to the enemy and that it was this which decided the issue of the battle. Since dysentery is far from uncommon among armies in the field, and since the Fulani horses may well have begun to be affected by the tsetse fly which infests the forests, this explanation, leaving aside both its supernatural element and the possibility of deliberate poisoning, carries conviction.

The completeness of the victory was demonstrated by the large numbers of prisoners and horses which were taken. These were the days 'when a horse could be bought in Oshogbo for one cowrie'. Only the tails were valued, as charms or decoration, and no attempt was made to use the captive horses to revive the Yoruba cavalry. Historians from Johnson onwards[1] have been puzzled that the Yoruba did not follow up their victory by counter-attacking towards the homelands in the north and instead pursued their internal wars. This is to look at history with the eyes of the present. The issues of the internal wars, political and economic, were real and profound. It was only when the advance of the British from Lagos was added to the aggression of the Fulani from the north and of the Dahomi from the west that internal reconciliation became feasible—too late.

[1] See, for example, Hodgkin, p. 47, and Crowder, p. 106.

VI

A TOWN ASSAULTED: THE BATTLE OF ABEOKUTA, 1851

The Dahomi attack on Abeokuta in 1851 was observed by Townsend, the Anglican missionary there, and Bowen, the American Southern Baptist (Burton's 'quondam Texas ranger'), both of whom have left written accounts of the engagement; there is also a Dahomian account as well as one by Johnson.[1] These authorities agree about the general course of the battle and, despite some minor disparities, supplement each other on the details.

The Dahomian troops left their capital at the end of February 1851, in the middle of the dry season. They were commanded by the *gaou* (general) Akati, and comprised some 10,000 male warriors and about 6,000 of the famous Amazons. After crossing the neutral Yoruba territory of Ketu, they passed through a village called Ekpo where an Egba spy gave them information about the weakest sectors in the defences of Abeokuta. On 2 March they attached Ishaga, an Egbado town some 12 miles south-west of Abeokuta. The ruler there submitted, and gave them apparently friendly advice to make the crossing of the river Ogun in daylight and to assault the neglected south-western walls of Abeokuta around the Aro gate; at the same time he sent a message to warn the Egba of the enemy's approach. Already apprized by their spies of the danger, the Egba were strengthening the walls at the threatened point and making other preparations. On 1 March Chief Somoye had been appointed Bashorun in succession to Apati (who had died two years before). Meanwhile Town-

---

[1] *C.M.I.*, 1851, pp. 165–6; Bowen, pp. 118–20; Dunglas (1949a); Johnson, pp. 313–16. See also Ajisafe, pp. 96–7. Townsend and Bowen both write of king Gezo of Dahomey as being present with his troops, but this appears to be mistaken.

send distributed the ammunition which Consul Beecroft had presented to the town on his visit the previous January with the instruction that it was to be used only for defensive purposes. The army, of some 15,000 men ('all armed with guns', wrote Bowen) and commanded by Sokenu, the Seriki, was now divided into three groups. Early on 3 March, as news came of the approach of the Dahomi, they moved into position. The first division took up its station by the river ford at Aro, about a mile from the town wall on the Badagry road. The second, under Chief Ogubonna (Balogun of Ikija and a great friend to the missionaries) crossed the river opposite the town, while the third held the area near the Aro gate.[1]

The Dahomi soon came into sight, moving in compact and disciplined bodies. While still to the west of the river, they divided into two parties, one advancing along the west bank to attack Ogubonna in the plain opposite the town walls, the other crossing the ford against light opposition from the Egba and then approaching the Aro gate over gradually rising ground.[2] The Egba vanguard, after failing to check the Dahomi at the ford, withdrew precipitately towards the protection of the south-west walls. This manœuvre, which may have been deliberate, led the enemy towards what had now been converted from the weakest to the strongest part of the defences. At first, however, the arrival at the Aro gate of the retreating vanguard caused dismay and confusion among the defenders there. Moreover, Ogubonna's men on the other side

[1] The site of the Aro gate (called by Bowen the 'Badagry gate') is in the Owu part of Abeokuta, near the Baptist and E.D.C. Secondary Modern Schools. A section of the remains of the wall may be seen to the east of the gate. The ford was probably at or near the point where the railway bridge now crosses the river; on the farther side is the village of Aro. Bowen, who describes the ford as being half a mile along the Badagry road, seems to have underestimated the distance.

[2] The ground between the Aro gate and the place where the Dahomi probably crossed the river is marshy for 200–300 yards from the river bank and then rises gradually towards the gate and southern walls. The Dahomian account by Dunglas is that the Dahomi followed the 'Aka ravine' when crossing this ground, but no place or stream of this name is now known in the area. The stream near Apo village, called locally the odo funfun ('white river'), would have provided no obstacle to the advance towards the gate.

of the river were seen to be giving ground before the advance of the Dahomi, and to the watchers on the wall they seemed likely to be in even greater difficulties as they retreated across the river where in this season there were still deep pools among the rocks. Bowen, who was standing near the gate, now persuaded the defenders at the wall to send down a detachment to cover Ogubonna, a measure which succeeded to the extent that Ogubonna's men were able to maintain their position on the farther side of the river. Meanwhile the other Egba troops, once inside the shelter of their walls, were showing greater determination and a rally took place in the neighbourhood of the gate. Townsend, who observed the battle through a telescope from a large rock inside the town, wrote afterwards that from the walls 'which were black with people, so heavy and well-sustained a fire was poured forth on the advancing enemy, that their progress was arrested'.

The battle along the walls continued throughout the day. The Egba, infuriated by the discovery (on preparing to castrate a captive) that many of their adversaries were women, redoubled their efforts, while their own women, led by the Iyalode, the redoubtable Madame Tinubu, formed a supply chain to bring up water, powder and food. By early evening, and after the repulse of ten full-scale attacks by them on the walls, the Dahomi realized that they had lost the day and began to withdraw. The Egba sent out a force to outflank them and also set fire to the high grass outside the walls, but the Dahomi succeeded in disengaging in good order, halting at intervals to discharge their muskets and slaughtering on their way some Egba farmers caught peacefully in their fields near the Ogun on the line of retreat. The next day the Dahomi fell upon Ishaga, but were now successfully taken in the rear by the Egba army and a second, hard battle was fought. The Egba skill and determination in defence were not, however, matched by equal qualities in the open field, and the Dahomi again succeeded in breaking off the battle and withdrew across their borders.

VII

SIEGE WARFARE: THE ORDEAL
OF IJAYE, 1860–2

The Ijaye war of 1860–2 exhibits many classic features of Yoruba warfare in the nineteenth century. It began as a struggle for pre-eminence between the two palatinates designated by Atiba some 30 years before: Ibadan, acting nominally in support of the Alafin, and Ijaye, the former with the great Ogunmola as its war leader and the latter still under the iron rule of Kurunmi, the Are.[1] It ended as a struggle between Ibadan and the Egba of Abeokuta who had intervened as allies of Ijaye. As well as accounts by Egba historians and by Johnson, there are contemporary descriptions of the war by Anglican and Baptist missionaries, and also Captain Jones's report based largely on his observation of the armies at Ijaye.[2]

The opening battles were fought between the Ibadan and the Ijaye in the forests between the two towns. After three sharp but indecisive engagements, the Ijaye ran short of ammunition and retired to the shelter of their walls.[3] By this time most of Yorubaland, including the Fulani at Ilorin, was joining in the war against the Ibadan who received little help from the Alafin's force encamped at Ilora, some 13 miles north of Ijaye. Only the Egba, resentful of Ibadan operations in an

[1] The Balogun of Ibadan at this time, and commander-in-chief of the Ibadan army at Ijaye, was Ibikunle. He had undertaken the war with reluctance in response to popular clamour. Ogunmola, later Bashorun, was already a more prominent and influential figure in the army.

[2] Ajisafe, pp. 109–11; Biobaku, ch. vi; Johnson, pp. 331–54; *C.M.I.*, 1862; *C.M.P.*, 1860–1 and 1861–2. For Captain Jones's report, see Appendix.

[3] Johnson writes (p. 338): 'The third and last battle fought before the arrival of the Egbas had exhausted the Are's store of ammunition.' But ammunition was generally made locally (although the metal was imported), so that it was perhaps the powder which was exhausted. Keeping the powder dry must also have been a great problem in these wars. During their siege of Ijaye the Ibadan depended for their ammunition upon the Alafin's blacksmiths at Oyo.

area where many of the Abeokuta peoples had their origin, gave effective support to Ijaye. An Egba army reached the beleaguered town in May 1860, securing its communications by establishing a camp at Olokemeji on the river Ogun, commanded by Ogunbonna.[1] The main army settled at leisure into a fortified camp south of the river Ose and not until after some weeks did they attempt to support their allies by taking the offensive. Then, in the first battle fought after the arrival of the Egba, the Ibadan gave clear evidence of their military superiority. They pursued the Egba and the Ijaye to the town gate where, however, they broke off the action, preferring to retire with their prisoners rather than to attempt to enter the town. A number of battles followed at intervals, fought in the plain beyond the Ose to the south of the town. In these engagements the Ibadan, who were better marksmen than the Egba and had learnt to reserve their fire, continued to have the upper hand, although still not to the point of attempting to storm the walls. One of these battles, on 23 May 1861, was observed from the Egba lines by Captain Jones who refers to it in his report as the 'battle of Ijaye'. Jones's experiences on this day provided the material for his comments on the command and handling of the Egba army.

The criticisms which occur in many parts of Jones's report are often presented by him as generalizations about the military methods and aptitude of the Yoruba. The limited nature of Jones's experience and evidence make this aspect of his report unconvincing. He did, however, appreciate that the Egba army which he saw in action in 1861 had declined since its victory over the Dahomi ten years before. He attributed this decline to the lack of vigour shown by the aged commander:[2]

---

[1] Ajisafe, p. 109, gives the date of arrival of the Egba at Ijaye as 5 June 1860; he implies that the detachment was sent to Olokemeji after this, whereas Johnson writes that the Olokemeji camp was established en route. The site of this camp is identified locally as being that of the old village of Olokemeji which was removed in 1923 about a mile to the north-east. The Ogun flows here between the eponymous two hills and the camp lay on the east bank of the river and on the southern flanks of the 'female hill'. Ruined walls and pottery may be discerned in the thick bush which covers the area.

[2] It is uncertain whether the commander described so scornfully by Jones

the fire of his eye and elasticity of frame is gone, while enervated by luxurious ease, lowered by the claims of his numerous wives, the gross effete old man passes his time in idleness and dissipation, instead of leading his dashing warriors to the fight. During the action of 23 May he never left his camp, and with such a commander the army is deserting in great numbers and a feeling of distrust has made serious inroads upon its efficiency.

In these circumstances the support of the Egba proved ruinous for the Ijaye. The once-powerful Are had become virtually the prisoner of his allies. Food and other supplies in the town ran low, and children were pledged to the Egba warriors who sent them to serve their households in Abeokuta. Ibadan next turned on the Oke Ogun (Upper Ogun) towns which were sending help to Ijaye, and captured the citadel of Iwawun where five of the Are's sons were taken and executed. The capture of Iwawun, where the upper town occupied the summit of a rock (or inselberg, characteristic of this district) rising steeply some 500 feet from the plain, was indeed a formidable undertaking. Moreover, the revelation by the war drums that the dread Ogunmola was present with the Ibadan force had a devastating effect on the defenders. The town was apparently never reoccupied after its destruction by the Ibadan.[1] Shortly afterwards the aged Kurunmi died. Meanwhile the Ibadan camp, established at Alabata some four miles to the south, was moved even nearer until it was fixed between the river Ose and the inner walls of the town. Privations increased for the Ijaye as the months went by. Stone, the Baptist missionary, had left for Abeokuta before the Are's death. Then a Lieutenant Dolbein from the Royal Navy succeeded in entering the town in order to escort the Anglican, the Rev. Adolphus Mann, and his ailing wife to Lagos. On

---

was Somoye the Bashorun (the more likely) or Anoba who bore the title of Kakanfo; see Johnson, p. 337; Biobaku, p. 66.

[1] Johnson's account of this capture (pp. 346–50) is largely confirmed by local accounts. Traces of the old town may be seen, and the inhabitants of the area point out sentry posts round the top of the rock, places where the strong natural defences were improved by earth walls and digging, and a platform commanding the approach to this acropolis, from which boulders were rolled at the enemy.

17 March 1862, the little party passed through the lines towards Abeokuta. The end had come. That evening the Egba abandoned their camp and their allies, and during the night the unfortunate Ijaye left their homes, most of them attempting to reach Abeokuta in the wake of the Egba. The following day, 18 March, the Ibadan entered the empty town. They set fire to its houses and decreed that it should never be rebuilt. A proverb still current in Ibadan asks: 'Is the salutation "Ijaye man" in front of Ogunmola's compound a greeting or a betrayal?' (*Akini je akini, afinihan je afinihan; ewo ni 'Ara Ijaye' l'ojude Ogunmola?*). A similar proverb in Abeokuta, substituting the name of Sodeke (the Seriki who led the Egba to Abeokuta) for Ogunmola, suggests that after the war the Ijaye were as unpopular with their former allies as with the Ibadan.

The main interest of this war is that after the opening stages it largely consisted in siege operations characteristic of Yoruba warfare. The visitor today to the walled cities of the Yoruba is confronted by the problem of how these sieges were conducted and the defence organized. The usually wide circuit of the walls precluded continuous manning, and the walls and ditches can hardly have been formidable obstacles in themselves to any determined enemy. Yet, as the battle of Abeokuta in 1851 shows, these fixed defences of the Yoruba did give to the defenders considerable advantages in morale and an increased effectiveness of fire. Thus attempts to assault the defences of a town were as rare (and when made, as rarely successful) as in the European wars of the sixteenth century. A night attack, which would probably have offered the best chance of success against a strong place, was still rarer, even after the Ibadan victory at Oshogbo had shown its value. In these circumstances the objective of an attacking army generally came to be the reduction of a besieged town by famine, as in the cases of Owu and Ijaye. This was often a lengthy undertaking as most towns had sources of water and farmland within their walls as well as friends outside. The greatest sufferers were the non-combatants.

VIII

OPEN WARFARE: THE BATTLE OF IKIRUN, 1878

The battle of Ikirun was a victory for the Ibadan over both the Fulani of Ilorin and a formidable coalition of most of the other Yoruba states. It was fought in the hills north-east of Oshogbo on 1 November 1878, when the rivers and streams of that region were in spate from the rains of the wet season then drawing to a close. The day was one in which a boldly planned offensive by the Ibadan met with an initial disaster which was turned to success by the determination and resource of the commander and the dash and endurance of his troops in a battle which ranged over a wide and difficult terrain. Johnson's account is detailed and vivid; his analysis of the fighting, descriptions of the engagements and understanding of the protagonists, especially the contrasted Ibadan leaders—the young and reckless Osi and the imperturbable but ailing Balogun—make one of the most splendid passages in this great history.[1]

Early in 1878 a number of the Ekiti rulers had taken advantage of Ibadan's preoccupation with the hostile Egba and Ijebu in the south to rebel against her predominance over them—a predominance which had been encouraged by Alafin Atiba's strategical dispositions 40 years before and which had developed into a form of empire since Ibadan's successes against the Fulani at Oshogbo and in the Ijaye war. The Ekiti began their rising by murdering the Ibadan *ajele* (political agents) in their towns. They were joined in their revolt by the people of Ila, and more reluctantly, by the Ijesha of Ilesha, and by June

---

[1] Johnson, pp. 427–36. Johnson's account was almost certainly based on information from participants in the battle, and it has been confirmed in outline from residents in Ikirun, Inisha and Iba.

the Ilorin had also entered the alliance. The movement, helped by the states in the south, now took on the aspect of a broad coalition whose first object was defined as the freeing of the towns between Ikirun and Iwo in order to confine the Ibadan to a boundary along the river Oba.[1]

The allies opened their hostilities against the town of Igbajo which had remained loyal to Ibadan. The leading chief in Ibadan, Latosisa the Are, did not at first take seriously this northern threat and continued to use his main force against the Egba, sending only a small detachment to help the Igbajo. But the Igbajo and Ibadan were soon forced to retreat to Ikirun, a town which had already become a place of refuge for the inhabitants of 28 lesser towns and which was now closely besieged by the allies. An urgent appeal was sent from Ikirun for help and at last, in October, the Are ordered the Balogun to lead out the main Ibadan army, which had just returned from raids against the Egba in the Meko district, to relieve the defenders of Ikirun.

The Ibadan army was commanded by the Balogun Ajayi Ogboriefon, a brave and experienced general but something of an intriguer and by now an ill man.[2] With him in his command the Are associated Ilori the Osi (a son of Ogunmola, Ibadan's great general in the Ijaye war). Ilori was still a young man and, despite his importance as the Balogun's deputy, had all the recklessness of youth. Under these leaders the army entered Ikirun on the last day of October. They learnt that the enemy were concentrated in three camps, the Ilorin some four and a half miles due north, the Ekiti together with the Ila encamped near to the Ilorin, and the Ijesha some four and a half miles to the north-east, within the small walled town of Iba whose inhabitants had fled to Ikirun. At a council of war held immediately on arrival the Balogun proposed to delay his attack for some days in order to rest the army after its

---

[1] The river Oba flows south from the area of Ogbomosho to join the Oshun about five miles east of Lalupon.

[2] Ajayi was known as Ogboriefon ('bearer of the Efon's head') because as a young soldier he had stalked and shot an Efon marksman, and brought back his enemy's head, holding it by the ear between his teeth.

long march. He planned then to divide his forces into two parts, leading the larger himself against the Ilorin and Ekiti camps while the Osi would attack the Ijesha with the other. The Osi argued against both these proposals, and the Balogun allowed him to have his way. It was therefore decided, in accordance with the Osi's plan, first that the army should launch its attack without delay the following morning and secondly that the Osi should take command of the left flank, as his office literally required, and thus of the major attack.

At dawn the next day the Osi, after despatching a bottle of gin, left the town by the northern (or Offa) gate, in advance of his own men who hurried to overtake him, and of his supporting war chiefs. After riding north for some three miles he turned aside into the bush, with the aim of taking the Ilorin in the rear. Those of his force who were in front of and behind him were left unaware of his action and pressed on towards the Ekiti camp. The Ekiti reacted sharply, overpowering Ilori's men and driving them back to the point where Ilori had entered the bush. They then practised a deception, sounding on their drums the war-cry of Akintola, a leading Ibadan chief (and son of the late Balogun Ibikunle) who had been left behind by Ilori's precipitate advance. Meanwhile the Ilorin, who had not known that the defenders of Ikirun had been reinforced, were faltering under Ilori's surprise attack. But the Osi, hearing the drums, broke off the engagement in anticipation of reinforcement, and the loss of impetus proved fatal. Alcohol had muddled him, and always a poor horseman, he lost control of his mount in the ensuing crisis and fell to the ground. His guards, whom he had antagonized by his arrogance, deserted him and he was ignominiously seized by the Ilorin.[1]

The Osi's followers were now captured or scattered. Some, however, succeeded in crossing the range of hills which separated them from the right flank of the army, which was now heavily engaged against the Ijesha, and told the Balogun

[1] The place where this occurred is identified as Agbe Shango, off the track from Iba to Ikirun.

what had happened. Ajayi ordered the bad news to be suppressed and straightway turned to attack an advancing company of the enemy. After taking a number of prisoners, he commanded them to be killed and then made a short tactical withdrawal. The main body of the Ijesha, coming suddenly upon their massacred comrades, halted in horror. The Balogun thereupon ordered a general charge. The enemy broke and the Ibadan drove into their camp at Iba. 'Let no one stay for booty or captives, all prisoners must be slain at once,' Ajayi cried. Ignoring a strong body of Ekiti on the flank, he now launched an attack on the Ilorin camp on the farther side of the Iba stream (or river Aisin). In this he was reinforced by the fresh troops of Akintola who had at last reached the battlefield and whose war-cry of *kiniun onibudo* ('the lion of the lord of the camps') was taken up by the whole army. The reinvigorated Ibadan plunged into the marshes of the river and threw themselves against the enemy. Taken aback by the onslaught, the Ilorin gave way and, staying only to slay their illustrious captive the Osi, and some lesser chiefs taken with him, fled towards Offa, while the Ekiti and Ila camps were quickly assaulted and taken. The defeated Ilorin were then pursued to the banks of the river Otin where they found that the bridge was broken—either from the force of the flood or by the action of people on the farther bank. There followed a desperate rush of men, women and horses into the swollen waters where many perished.

The incident led to this battle being called the Jalumi ('rush into the water') war. The place where the stampede occurred was almost certainly where the old road from Iba to Okuku crossed the river Otin by a wooden bridge.[1] The river here

[1] The site of this bridge is about 2½ miles south-east of Okuku and 100 yards east of the railway line to Offa. The place of the stampede was marked by two concrete pillars erected in the stream by Oyekunle, a previous Olokuku of Okuku; these have now collapsed. It is commonly believed in Ikirun, however, that the Jalumi episode occurred near the girder bridge over the Otin on the present main road from Ikirun to Offa. This would imply that the Ilorin had first retreated south across the Aisin and then south-west to the Otin, which is unlikely. Confusion has probably arisen because Captain Bower, the first British Resident in Ibadan, camped nearby in 1896 when engaged in opera-

runs between banks about 15 feet high and is said to flood in the wet season to this depth.[1]

There are contradictory accounts of the destruction of the bridge in the rear of the Ilorin. Johnson writes that it was deliberately cut by the Offa, and Hermon-Hodge that an Ibadan man named Kaniki was in Offa and persuaded the people there to take this action.[2] The present Egburu of Iba, however, was told by his father, who took part in the battle, that the bridge was borne away by a sudden swelling of the river. (The Ibadan are said to have contrived this flood by vexing the river goddess, putting millet, a dog and a pig into the water: they were then able to continue their advance by crossing the river on the corpses of the drowned enemy.)[3] Again, the people of Okuku and Erin (large villages between the Otin and Offa) both claim that it was their men who broke the bridge, while in Ikirun it is said that a detachment from the beleaguered town itself crossed the river and cut the bridge on the day of the battle. The rest of the defeated allies presumably fled to the south-west, separating themselves from the Ilorin.

This crushing victory had been won by the Ibadan by methods which contrast strongly with the deliberate and cautious operations, practised for example at Ijaye, which characterized much of Yoruba warfare in this century. At Ikirun the Ibadan had chosen to make a surprise attack on two widely separated fronts, planned and co-ordinated to a degree which, in the absence of maps and clocks, was remarkable. In the execution they had shown both persistence and a talent for improvization. But, as sometimes happens in war, success in the field proved not to alter greatly the political situation. The

---

tions against the Ilorin, and placed a small artillery piece here as a monument and a warning to the Fulani.

[1] However, on 4 November 1962, after an unusually wet season, the river a few miles below this point was only four feet deep at the centre and could easily be forded.

[2] Johnson, p. 434; Hermon-Hodge, p. 71.

[3] Much the same account as that by the Egburu was given by an elderly chief at Offa, and also by Mr. Paul Alatayo of Ikirun, and Oparinu, Arin Oje of Inisha; the last two were both born about 1870 and have some recollection of the battle.

Ijebu declined Ibadan's offer of alliance, the Ilorin continued
to threaten Offa (which hindered their movement southward), and the Egba still barred the roads to the coast; even
the Ekiti and Ijesha were defiant and, broadening the basis of
their coalition, formed the confederation known as the Ekiti-
parapo. The situation of Ibadan remained critical, and in
April of the following year, to the city's misfortunes was added
the death in his house of the Balogun Ajayi, the hero of Ikirun.

IX

CASUALTIES AND CAPTIVES:
THE IMPACT OF THE WARS

The battles at Abeokuta and Ikirun, and at least some of the engagements in the Ijaye war, were fought with a ferocity and determination which make it difficult to accept Burton's contention that the casualties suffered in the wars were trifling, even though the claims of dead, wounded and captured passed down from the combatants are doubtless exaggerated.[1] It does seem that the introduction of firearms, which until the appearance of the Sniders in the 1870's were of a primitive type, and the decline of close-fighting, led to a decrease in the number of fatalities in battle. Jones wrote, somewhat scornfully, that 'tho' thousands of rounds be fired, the killed may be counted by units and the wounded by tens. Seventeen thousand men engaged in mortal combat on May 23rd. [1861], the killed on both sides, as ascertained by spies, were 5 and the wounded under 50!' Yet this suggestion of a kind of Renaissance warfare is at variance with the evidence of the missionaries who not only were often observers but were also concerned in succouring the wounded—or even, in Bowen's case, in helping occasionally with operations.[2] Townsend wrote that after the attack on Abeokuta in 1851 1,200 Dahomi dead were counted along the walls after that one day's fighting and he estimated the total casualties among the Dahomi at 3,000

[1] Burton (1863), p. 295. See also Burton's evidence to the 1865 Select Committee on Africa, whom he told that the Africans of these parts 'go out to fight, and as soon as a man is killed they retire for the day'.

[2] The Egba also had the assistance in the Ijaye war of two American negroes, Vaughan and Pettiford. They had come to Yorubaland from Liberia, where they had been carpenters, and were members of the Southern Baptist mission. Johnson (p. 353) refers to them as 'Afro-American sharp-shooters'. In the Iperu war a few months later Pettiford nearly succeeded in picking off Ogunmola himself.

(where Bowen estimated 2,000), with some 1,000 taken captive.[1] At Ijaye, Mann was at times dealing daily with some 40 to 60 wounded soldiers in his dispensary at the Anglican mission, and his talent as an amateur surgeon was in demand. Stone also refers to casualties at Ijaye as being considerable, adding that wounds inflicted by the iron or copper bullets tended to become gangrenous. Johnson recounts that between April 1860 and March 1862 in the Ijaye war Ogunmola alone lost 1,800 of his soldier slaves, excluding losses among his free followers—a figure derived from counting the caps of the fallen which had been preserved in a huge basket.[2] It seems beyond doubt, therefore, that on occasion—both before and after the introduction of firearms—casualties were numerous and serious, and Burton's attempt, on slender evidence, to minimize the determination with which these wars were fought must be rejected. Even so, the toll of life among non-combatants in the wars seems likely to have been at least as high as that among the warriors, whether from famine, as at Ijaye and Owu, or by the unprovoked slaughter of those unlucky enough to be caught in the track of the armies, like the Egba farmers along the river Ogun.

The fate of those who were captured provides a further problem. Clearly, the taking of prisoners was an important aim of the combatants; in at least one action at Ijaye the Ibadan so encumbered themselves with captives that they were unable to press home a victory which might have won them the town some months earlier than its eventual fall.[3] It has been assumed, and still seems probable, that captives from the wars provided the bulk of the slaves exported via the markets of Dahomey and the Lagos lagoon, and this has led to the further assumption that the wars were themselves occasioned

[1] *C.M.I.*, 1851, pp. 162–7. Burton (1864) observed that 'king Gezo lost the flower of his force [of Amazons] under the walls of Abeokuta'; their loss was still felt in 1863.

[2] *C.M.P.*, 1860–1, pp. 50–2; Stone, ch. XVIII; Johnson, p. 354. The corpses of the dead seem usually to have been left on the field of battle, to be devoured by vultures and other wild animals.

[3] Stone, ch. XVIII.

by the demand for slaves. This overlooks the important political and economic issues of the wars, and the most that can yet be said in this connexion is that the supply of slaves was greatly increased and that the appetite for taking captives who could be profitably disposed of in this way probably prolonged particular campaigns and may also have prolonged the general state of warfare.

By no means all those enslaved were sold overseas. The majority probably served to satisfy the local demand for slaves, which had paradoxically been increased by the growth of 'legitimate' trade with its call for porters to carry the palm products to the coast.[1] Moreover, not all captives were enslaved. Some were imprisoned, like Stone's interpreter Thomas, who was captured at Ijaye and kept in irons at Ibadan for three years, dying soon after his release.[2] The least fortunate were put to death, like those Dahomi prisoners who suffered at the hands of the Egba in 1851 in revenge for the slaughter by their retreating comrades of the Egba farmers. The most fortunate were redeemed or even released freely; after the defeat of the Dahomi in 1851, for example, large numbers of captives were taken by the Egba to Ketu and handed over there to their countrymen against payment, and many of the Ijaye taken after the fall of their town were surreptitiously freed by their kinsmen in Ibadan.[3] Bowen relates that one of the prisoners was a girl warrior who had been born in Ketu (and so was almost certainly a Yoruba) and captured in early life by the Dahomey. This Amazon, when brought to Ketu, refused to allow her parents to buy her freedom, preferring to return to the service of Dahomey.[4]

Finally there is the problem of the degree to which the social and economic life of Yorubaland was dislocated by the wars.

---

[1] Burton told the Select Committee in 1865 that on the West Coast 'The man is bought for a few shillings, and sent up to collect palm oil'. The export of slaves from the area had fallen away completely but 'the demand for domestic slavery has increased, which tends greatly to the misery of the slaves' (PP, 1865, v (412), QQ.2165–6).

[2] Stone, ch. xxiv.   [3] Ajisafe, p. 97; Johnson, p. 352; Bowen, pp. 148–9.

[4] Bowen, pp. 148–9.

It is generally accepted that devastation and depopulation were widespread. Certainly the misery occasioned by the prolonged warfare must have been considerable. Armies marched and counter-marched across the land, or undertook sieges which might last many months, living all the time mainly on what they could take from the local farms. There was not much greater security for life than for property in their vicinity; Lander, after his journey in 1830, wrote of the ruined and abandoned towns which he had seen still prosperous only a few years before when travelling by the same road with Clapperton.[1] To some extent, the accounts of the missionaries —Stone, Bowen, the Hinderers, for example—sustain the dismal picture at a later period. Despite this, however, the effect of the wars on the ordinary life of the countryside may not have been great. It seems likely that in the smaller towns and villages of the bush, remote from the tracks connecting the towns which were the main protagonists, and along which the armies moved, the farmers planted and harvested their crops and led their lives in community as unconscious of the great events being enacted around them as were the peasants of England during the civil wars of the fifteenth and seventeenth centuries.

[1] Lander, chs II and III.

X

THE MILITARY AND POLITICAL ACHIEVEMENT

This account of the warfare of the Yoruba in the nineteenth century is preliminary and tentative. Much remains to be done in compiling and comparing the records and traditions of the individual kingdoms, and there may well be much to learn about these wars from Fulani and Dahomey sources. Problems will arise in addition to those to which answers have been suggested in this essay. Yet the evidence seems already strong enough to refute that commonly held view that these wars were fought in an air of unreality and with little danger to the contestants by demoralized armies whose organization, command and equipment were so primitive that they can be said to have practised neither strategy nor tactics. Burton's account of the Egba army, which propagates this view, is little more than a jaundiced version of Captain Jones's report. This report is in fact a serious and by no means unfavourable appraisal, and many of its criticisms are of only limited application.[1] It confirms what emerges from other sources; that the Yoruba had by the early nineteenth century evolved a complex and flexible military organization which now succeeded in adapting itself to the changes occasioned by the introduction of firearms into general use. The source of these military concepts of the Yoruba and their relation to those of other African peoples—and perhaps also the Portuguese—is a problem of great interest, but beyond the scope of this essay.

Nor can these wars be dismissed as slave raids or as petty civil strife. They concerned, and came near to settling, two

---

[1] Jones's conventional reference in his report to 'the irregular marching and skirmishing of a barbarous horde' reads incongruously after his objective consideration of the merits and weakness of the Egba army.

profound political issues: first, the menace to the whole people from two formidable external enemies, and then the rival claims to power of individual Yoruba kingdoms after the decline and eclipse of Oyo—and they were fought with the hardihood which political conviction engenders. Though the external issue seems now the more important, the Yoruba of the nineteenth century can hardly be blamed for failing to appreciate this. By the time that the wars entered their final stage, the external threat had been countered; after 1864 the Dahomi never again assaulted a Yoruba capital. Still more important, the withdrawal of the Yoruba to the south, from the late 1820's onwards, and their victory at Oshogbo in *c.* 1840, had effectively checked the Fulani. This success served to sharpen the internal issue and to stimulate the combinations directed mainly against Ibadan, which had emerged as the most powerful of the successor states. When the British intervened in the last decade of the century it was not, as is sometimes suggested, to save in the nick of time a shattered people from the advance of the *jihad*, but to impose their *pax* on states which were still prosecuting a war among themselves for political and economic predominance in which the Fulani were less a common enemy than a convenient ally to one or other side.

PART II

THE IJAYE WAR
1860–1865

I

INTRODUCTORY

There are many reasons why a detailed study of the Ijaye War is important. The first is the abundance of the material, both the written evidence of contemporary eye-witnesses and the oral tradition recorded at different times. This makes the Ijaye War unique among the great events of African history before the establishment of European rule. Usually, material is so fragmentary that we have to substitute theories—both naïve and perceptive theories of 'primitive society' and Man in the abstract—for evidence of the action and motives of men. But here the material is such that the story of the war and the character, actions and motivations of the main participants can be examined in some considerable detail. This in turn may affect some of our theories of 'primitive society'.

Secondly, as Clausewitz has said, war 'is only a part of political intercourse . . . a continuation of political intercourse with a mixture of other means.'[1] Therefore a detailed history of a few years of war becomes a significant mirror of the politics of the age. In the intense activities of war, useful light is thrown on the pattern of life, the pattern of authority and especially on the pattern of external relations. This is true of wars in general, but particularly true of the Ijaye War which occupies a central place in the turbulent history of the Yoruba in the nineteenth century. It was, in a sense, the climax of the struggle to re-establish the order which had broken down when the Old Oyo empire collapsed at the beginning of the century. The importance of the war can be judged from the ramification of alliances which came to involve practically all the Yoruba states including Ilorin and, to a lesser or greater extent Borgu, Dahomey, Benin, Nupe and Ashanti. European

[1] See Greene (ed.), p. 108. See also Fuller, pp. 59–76.

powers also became involved, the British directly and the French indirectly.

The abundance of contemporary written evidence is due to the fact that missionaries of various societies in different parts of Yoruba and Dahomey took great interest in the war because they realized its importance to the future of their different spheres of activities. Apart from peripheral sources from groups in Lagos, including the British administration there, and Catholic missionaries at Whydah and Porto Novo, the main evidence is from Anglican, Methodist and American Baptist missionaries living at the main centres of the war, Ibadan, Ijaye, Abeokuta and Oyo.[1] This evidence was of course coloured by the external view and the special interests of the missionaries. But, with the exception of those at Ijaye who had never been made to feel at home, the missionaries tended to identify themselves with the communities among whom they lived and worked, and they saw issues mostly from the point of view of those particular communities.

Thus, the Anglican missionary at Ibadan talked of the Egba seeking to get the Ijebu to trouble 'us', meaning the Ibadan. He saw God taking an interest on the side of Ibadan because, as he said, 'As long as Ilorin stands a Mohammedan power in this country, it is by no means to be wished that Ibadan's war power should diminish, or the Yoruba country would be overrun with Mohammedanism and Christian missions be at an end.'[2] On the other hand, the leading Anglican missionary at Abeokuta, with the concurrence of the Methodist missionary there, saw God participating actively on the side of the Egba. 'The Egbas', he said, 'are the power that represents progress and advancing civilization, and it is to be feared if they should be conquered, our cause, or rather that of God, would suffer at least for a time immensely.'[3] Queried as to why his evidence contradicted so vigorously that of his colleagues at Ijaye, the Baptist missionary at Oyo replied: 'Statements about the war

[1] See Bibliography I(b).
[2] Hinderer to Venn, 26 Aug. 1860, 2 Aug. 1861 (C.M.S. CA2/049).
[3] Townsend to Venn, 4 Oct. 1860 (C.M.S. CA2/085).

made by them and by myself may appear contradictory, but it must be remembered that we are differently situated and obtain our information from different sources. I think the missionaries at Ijaye and Abeokuta are deceived to some extent.'[1]

However much they might have puzzled the various committees in London and Richmond (Virginia, U.S.A.) trying to advise their missionaries as to what policies to adopt in the war, these contradictions enhance the value of the evidence for the historian. The missionaries became so involved in the war that to a remarkable extent they shed their external points of view and became spokesmen of the combatants. That is not to say, however, that the written evidence is sufficient. Apart from the absence of internal evidence from any of the non-Yoruba states, what we have from the missionaries are despatches of special correspondents from the main theatres of the war, not the private diaries of the generals or minutes of the war councils.

The nearest we get to these internal sources, as summed up and modified by group memory, is handed down as oral tradition. The recording of this, though by no means complete, is satisfactory. Samuel Johnson began to collect material for his *History of the Yorubas* within 20 years of the Ijaye War. He recognized the full significance of the war, and devoted 36 pages of some of his best prose to it.[2] From his account we can hear the very sounds of the war drums of Kurunmi of Ijaye and Balogun Ibikunle of Ibadan, significant sounds which the ears of most missionaries missed. To what extent Johnson's *History* has itself become a source of 'oral tradition' will make interesting research. But when I worked with the Yoruba Historical Research Scheme on the oral tradition of the war as it exists today, we often heard Johnson quoted. There seemed to be little remembered to supplement his account in the general story of the war. There are, however, songs and praise verses preserved in the families of the leading personalities, which could add detailed touches here and there. There are

[1] Reid to Poindexter, 3 Sept. 1860 (S.B.C.). [2] Johnson, pp. 328–64.

traditions in the farming villages which add local details, but the variations they suggest seem to reflect present-day political attitudes as much as authentic history. Traditions in Ijebu-Remo also give significant details of the later stages of the war, where Johnson is very brief. All these and those recorded in the local history books of Ibadan, Abeokuta and Ijebu I have used in this work. There is however need for more work on the oral tradition of the war in Ijebu Ode, Ilorin and the non-Yoruba states.

II

ANTECEDENTS

The Ijaye War had its origin in the rivalry of the different successor states of the Old Oyo empire, trying to fill the power
vacuum created when the empire collapsed. Old Oyo had
maintained peace in the more open country of Northern
Yoruba as well as on both sides of the river Ogun among the
Egba and Egbado, and westwards in Dahomey. It did not
directly control the eastern Yoruba states of the more forested
areas like Ife, Ilesha, Ekiti, Ondo and Ijebu, but it had a working arrangement with them, based on the belief of a common
origin at Ile-Ife for all the leading Yoruba *obas*. It was because of the effectiveness of this arrangement that the Yoruba
did not feel the full impact of the disruptive influences of
the slave trade till the 1820's.[1] But even before the end of the
eighteenth century, the arrangement was already breaking
down because of internal disruptions at the heart of the empire.

The Oyo-speaking peoples of the metropolitan area of the
empire became divided in their loyalty to the Alafin. There was
a prolonged constitutional conflict when the *Basorun*, leader of
the council of senior chiefs, disputed power with successive
Alafins. Various towns and provinces in the empire began to
take sides, some for the Basorun, others for the Alafin. Rivalries and feuds developed between towns, classes of chiefs,
families and individual leaders. The Egba seized the opportunity of this conflict at the centre of the empire to expel the
resident officials of the Alafin and to declare themselves independent. Towards the end of the century, Alafin Abiodun had
a fair measure of success in patching up the situation. He succeeded in destroying the over-mighty Basorun and most of his
relatives, and he tried to restore order. But the divisions in the

---

[1] Biobaku, pp. 12–13.

body politic had gone deep. They soon reappeared when Abiodun was followed in quick succession by a number of ineffective Alafins. Thus, when Dahomey took the chance in 1818 to throw off Oyo rule, it met little resistance. When Afonja, the Are-ona-Kakanfo, the leading general, invited the Fulani to aid his rebellion in Ilorin, and the Fulani seized the opportunity to extend the Muslim *jihad* to the Yoruba country, they found the people and their rulers hopelessly divided. From about 1825 until they were defeated at the battle of Oshogbo in 1840, Ilorin armies destroyed most of the northern Oyo towns. They raided Old Oyo itself, cut off its supplies and forced the Alafin to abandon it and seek a new capital. Masses of the population migrated southwards. Towns like Ogbomosho and Iwo became swollen in size with Oyo refugees; the overflow began to settle on Ife and Egba farms. Migrant Oyo warriors in alliance with Ife and Ijebu people destroyed Owu and practically all the Egba towns and villages. They settled on their land and pushed the Egba farther to the south. In the upheaval, several leaders were thrown up who undertook energetically the task of town building and reconstruction. New towns and new centres of political power arose, notably Ibadan and Ijaye in the old Egba country, Modakeke next door to Ile-Ife, and Abeokuta southwards on the banks of the river Ogun.

The break-up of the Old Oyo empire had posed the question of what was to take its place. This was the grand question of nineteenth-century Yoruba history. A quick and decisive answer would have made all the difference. But in such a crisis, the immediate concern of the people was not to find answers to grand questions but to survive. With the central authority gone, and no one single leader gaining dominance, the responsibility for organizing defence fell on the individual major towns. To organize defence, they tried to carve out little empires of their own, bringing the smaller towns and villages under their control and levying tribute on them. From units of local government, each taking its place within a monarchical structure, the major towns were seeking to become capitals of rival states with rival loyalties and patriotisms. In this way, 'the love of town came to supplant the love of country.'[1] As a result, the rivalries of the towns expressed in times past usually in the gentle rivalries of their *obas* and *bales* for precedence began to be expressed in bloody wars of survival. That is not to say that the grand question of restoring order in the country as a whole was lost sight of, but that the immediate concern of each town for survival made them resist the ambitions of any other town aspiring to take the place of Old Oyo.

Wars have a logic of their own, a built-in vicious circle which provides in each war a reason for another. The break down of central authority provoked the necessity for each section to defend itself. Each section, acting in self-defence, prevented the re-emergence of central authority; and without a central authority, the necessity for each section to organize its own defence could not be removed. The wars encouraged increasing use of imported flint-lock guns, gunpowder and other European weapons. Soon, these imported weapons displaced home-made implements like matchets, clubs, bows and arrows, as armaments for the ordinary soldier. From being occasional interruptions from farming, war was becoming the regular pre-occupation of a new class of people who had to organize the supply of these weapons and ensure the control of the trade routes through which they came. This increased the importance of semi-professional war chiefs to a degree hitherto unknown in the Yoruba country. The ambitions of these chiefs themselves often precipitated war. Their bid for political power encouraged innovations and new constitutional experiments at variance with the traditional ideas of government. There was often conflict, taking different forms in different towns, between these new classes of war chiefs and the traditional civil authorities. This further unsettled Yoruba politics; and by undermining what was left of the monarchical principle and the traditional conventions for adjusting inter-group relationships in the Yoruba country, it made the search for peace even more difficult.

[1] Oyerinde, p. 101.

Nobody was more conscious of the importance of the traditional principles and conventions than Atiba who had succeeded to the title of Alafin in about 1837. At the new capital, also named Oyo, he worked patiently to regain the power of his ancestors. He had been a wild dissolute young prince. At one stage in his career, he had befriended the Fulani at Ilorin and claimed to be a convert to Islam or 'tapped the Koran' as the phrase was. But as Alafin, he turned to tradition as the only possible restorer of order. He replanned and rebuilt the new capital. He was said to have brought people forcibly from the surrounding villages to enlarge it. At the centre of it, he built himself a fine palace, a copy of that at Old Oyo, with the traditional *Kobis*[1] and as many of the ornaments as he could recover from the old palace. He set up a well-ordered court full of splendour and colour and proceeded to impress upon everybody around that it was rebellion that broke the old kingdom, and if further disaster was to be avoided, there was to be only one master in the kingdom. But he was to be master not by physical force—which Atiba did not possess—but by virtue of tradition, the old sacred dignity of the throne, the spiritual force that was the ultimate safeguard of the monarchy. All the old offices were to be filled, the old ceremonies and court ritual meticulously and elaborately observed. The king was no longer to go to war. He was to remain aloof, mysterious, but alert and patient, and in the end, by astute diplomacy, he would win. Those in the kingdom who possessed physical force would soon realize that they would only destroy one another with it if they did not come to lay it before the traditional head and only use it at his bidding. He was a tall, charming, soft-spoken man, an imaginative conservative, a little pathetic in his undying belief in the force of tradition in a world of revolutionary changes.[2] After all, the Old Oyo empire was not

---

[1] A type of gables, a special architectural feature of royal courtyards in the Yoruba country, and restricted to royal courtyards only.

[2] See letters and journals of Hinderer (C.M.S. CA2/049), passim; in particular 17–23 January 1856, 30 May 1856, 9 Aug. 1858. Atiba never lost an opportunity to emphasize to his audience the importance of tradition and authority. Shown a musical box, for the first time, he listened carefully to the

just a traditional tribal state. Ife, not Oyo, was the mythical home of the Yoruba of whom the Oyo were just a branch, and not the senior branch. The power Atiba's predecessors wielded derived not only from the ancestors, but also from Oyo's geographical position, from its cavalry force and administrative system, and it was unlikely that an appeal to tradition alone could restore it.

The warriors who had taken refuge at Ijaye and Ibadan were a little more realistic. The kingdom, they felt, had to be conquered and ruled by effort and determination, not by wishful thinking. They proceeded to put this into practice, and though nominally acknowledging the Alafin's suzerainty, they continued to struggle with one another to see which of them would exercise the reality of power 'on his behalf'.

At Ijaye, Kurunmi 'the greatest Yoruba general and tactician of the day'[1] who succeeded to the title of Are-ona-Kakanfo established a personal ascendancy. He was king, judge, general, entertainer, sometimes also executioner. All refugees in the town had to submit to his will or quit. He was shrewd, cheerful, cynical, authoritarian; casual and generous to his friends, but implacable and unscrupulous where his enemies were concerned. He bolstered up his power not only by judicious feasting of the masses every fifth day but also by usurping the headship of the different cults, particularly that of Sango. Indeed, he was said to have been feared more than the Gods. To a man who refused to worship Sango, he said, 'If Sango does not kill you, I myself will'. And it was current saying in his time 'If the Are [as he was generally referred to] calls and you say you are busy consulting the oracle, what if the oracle says well and the Are says ill?' In this authoritarian way, he built up an army from among his followers and proceeded to conquer the *Ekun Otun*, the provinces of the Old Oyo

---

music and then called the attention of his entourage to the deep bass like the master drum in a Yoruba ensemble: 'Oh now listen, there is a master inside that music! How wonderful, everybody and everything in the world has a master' (Hinderer, Journal entry for 30 May 1856).

[1] Johnson, p. 282.

67

empire to the west of the upper Ogun, and to tax the people heavily for the upkeep of his army. He accepted from Atiba the title of Are-Ona-Kakanfo, with special commission to protect the western boundary of the kingdom from the Dahomey who, following their independence, were beginning to make inroads into the Yoruba country. But Kurunmi appeared to have been building up a kingdom for himself while keeping a watchful eye on the activities of Ibadan to the east.[1] By 1851 his officials claimed he was 'the owner' of all the upper Ogun 'almost to Saki'.[2]

At Ibadan no one chief was supreme. Under Oluyole, the Oyo refugees gained control of the town from their Ife and Ijebu allies. Like Kurunmi, he too aspired to a personal autocracy, but there were too many powerful personalities in Ibadan, and Oluyole died relatively young in 1847. What emerged after a period of experimenting was an attempted compromise between the ideas of the war chiefs demanding a military autocracy suitable to war camps, and the ideas of civil chiefs who wanted a traditional conciliar form of government. There were two parallel lines of chiefs, one civil, the other military. Titles were not tied to particular lineages, but were open to talent, merit and personal influence, through a system of promotion. When the most senior chief was a man who had risen through the ranks of civil chiefs, he took the title of Bale. If he had risen through the military line, he took the title of Basorun or Are-ona-Kakanfo. In theory, the civil chiefs took precedence over their corresponding war chiefs. In practice, it was the war chiefs who exercised the weightier influence over politics (for example, over issues of promotion and discipline of chiefs, policy towards Oyo and other states, the declaration of and the conduct of wars). In short, though Ibadan continued to recognize the suzerainty of the Alafin, it was largely an autonomous republic ruled by a military oligarchy. The

---

[1] See especially Mann to Venn, 20 July 1853, 23 Feb. 1853, 8 Feb. 1854 (C.M.S. CA2/066). Also Townsend, Journal for Aug. 1852, Sept. 1852, Jan. 1854 (C.M.S. CA2/085); Stone, pp. 53–7, 176, 223–4.

[2] Bowen, p. 161.

class of chiefs trained their young men in war and set their slaves and prisoners of war to cultivate their farms. Agriculture was a lowly and war a noble profession; manliness and courage being the two virtues most highly honoured and respected, even in an enemy. With its central position, and alliances with coastal states like Ijebu, Porto Novo and Benin, Ibadan made sure of a regular supply of guns and gunpowder.[1]

Following the battle of Oshogbo, the Ibadan began gradually to reconquer from Ilorin the Old Oyo provinces east of the Ogun, as far north as Offa; then they turned east towards the Ijesha, Ekiti and Akoko countries. At each place they conquered they appointed an Ajele (a resident official much like the Muslim district head, responsible to one of the war chiefs at Ibadan) to supervise the local rulers and collect tax. To bring back the old glory of the kingdom, they offered a centralized administration and a standing army based on Ibadan. But force had its limitations. Ibadan had no monopoly of the sources of ammunition. And, as Atiba feared, Ibadan and Ijaye soon became jealous rivals. In 1844 a quarrel led to a pitched battle at Batedo. Atiba intervened, sending the emblems of Sango to the two camps, implying that if the contestants did not respect him, they would probably respect his deified ancestor. The warriors decamped, but that was not the end of their rivalry.

The Egba had no ambition to reconquer the kingdom from which they had seceded in the middle of the eighteenth century.[2] Pushed out of their old home, they sought new opportunities to the south. Sodeke, himself once a refugee at Ibadan, began about 1830 to gather the remnants of some of the 153 Egba towns and villages in the three sectional groups of Ake, Oke Ona and Agura. He added a fourth group, the Owu who though ethnically closer to the Oyo, had suffered a fate similar to the Egba's. Sodeke was an able leader of men, 'of a

[1] Johnson (1937); Akinyele; also the letters and journals of Hinderer, resident at Ibadan 1853–64 (C.M.S. CA2/049).
[2] Biobaku, ch. II.

large powerful frame, and rather corpulent',[1] genial and warm-hearted, a patriotic soldier rather than an ambitious politician. He led the Egba through a revolution of considerable magnitude without leaving an imprint on their political organization. His leadership was personal and he addressed himself mostly to the external problems of defence.

To start with, the greatest threat to Abeokuta came from the Ijebu. In 1832, aided by Ibadan, the Ijebu had in fact nearly wiped out the new town when Adele I, the exiled Oba of Lagos living at Badagry, came to its aid with arms and troops. Sodeke saw that if the Egba were to survive, they must have direct access to ammunition from the coast, gain a port of their own, and make contacts with the European world. Badagry, weak and divided, was his obvious choice. He therefore sought to control the Egbado and Awori people who lived between Abeokuta and Badagry. He conquered Otta and Ilaro, laid siege to Ado and welcomed missionaries to Abeokuta. He did not develop any machinery for the effective government of the conquered places, only insisting that the rulers should be people favourable to the Egba, and who would welcome them and give them land to farm and protect their traders to and from the coast. Within the walls of Abeokuta, the different groups and towns continued to maintain their traditional rulers as if they were still physically separate or, as a missionary later said, 'as if the German principalities and little kingdoms were brought together in one town, each acting but seldom in unison'.[2] Sodeke died in 1844. Okukenu, a leading Ogboni chief, assumed something like a regency over the town under the title of Sagbua. Ten years later he was crowned Alake, with effective power largely in Ake alone. On his death in 1862, Somoye, a leading war chief, again assumed a regency and it was not till his death in 1868 that the Egba began to grapple with the necessity to work out an effective constitution. The problems of the Egba con-

---

[1] Freeman (1882), pp. 360–8. Also Freeman (1844); Townsend, Journal while on a Mission of Research, Jan. 1843 (C.M.S. CA/0215).

[2] Townsend to Commander Wilmot, 5 Aug. 1851 (PP 1852 LIV), p. 157.

stitution were at least in part a mirror of the malaise in the whole Yoruba country resulting from the imbalance between the traditional civil and the new military classes—between the *Ogboni* and the *Ologun*.

Meanwhile, the Ijebu had been watching developments in the interior of the Yoruba country with the eyes of shrewd businessmen. They controlled the coastal trade between Lagos and Benin. The wars in the interior meant both a plentiful supply of slaves and an increasing demand for guns and gunpowder. And they did a roaring trade in the 1820's and 1830's. They joined in the foundation of Ibadan and saw the rise of Abeokuta with its ambitions towards the coast as a threat to their position. By the 1850's, however, they began to see the situation differently.[1] They had been expelled from Ibadan and Ibadan was getting increasingly powerful, a potentially more dangerous threat than the Egba had been. The Ibadan were still good customers. This economic factor as well as internal divisions among the Ijebu themselves began to complicate their reaction to the growing power of Ibadan. In particular, many towns in Ijebu Remo were trying to throw off the overlordship of the Awujale, and the Ibadan, seeing in Ikorodu their most direct access to the sea, began to encourage the Remo secessionist movement. Gradually, Ijebu Ode and Ijebu Igbo were finding themselves in sympathy with the Egba in their conflict against Ibadan.

While Ijebu Ode became more friendly to the Egba, Dahomey emerged as Abeokuta's most implacable foe. The very area to the west of the lower Ogun, down to the coast, in which the Egba were spreading their influence and power became the focus of Dahomey's ambition. Dahomey began by aiding the different Egbado and Awori towns attacked by the Egba.

[1] The first report of the Ibadan/Ijebu Ode split was in 1857 when the British Consul in Lagos reported that Ijebu traders at the Ibadan market were seized, and communication between both towns was broken. (Campbell to Clarendon, 1 July 1857, P.R.O., F.O. 84/1031). In October 1860, the Consul sent to Ijebu Ode to find out on which side they were in the war. They declared that they were on the Egba side. (Hand to Russell, 9 Oct. 1860.) But up till then they had shown it so little that it was necessary to ask them.

In particular, they supported Ado, besieged since 1840, and the Egba had to give up the siege after 13 years. Open clash between Dahomey and the Egba was inevitable. It came first (at a small village called Imojulu) in 1844 when an Egba contingent from Ado ambushed the Dahomey army on their way to attack Ilaro and captured the royal seat and umbrella of king Gezo who then swore by his ancestors, whose emblems were so humiliated, that he would destroy Abeokuta. He made the next move in 1848 by destroying Oke Odan to clear the way. The Egba replied in 1850 by sacking Igbeji, a Dahomey outpost.[1] Gezo then ordered an attack on Abeokuta itself. This took place in 1851 with a large army of about 12,000 which was heavily defeated under the walls of Abeokuta.[2] It was an effective repulse and Gezo was to make no other such attempt to avenge his insulted ancestors. That was left to his dutiful son, Glele, who succeeded him in 1858 and made the destruction of Abeokuta his most important objective.

Finally, there was Ife to consider, still wielding considerable spiritual force in the Yoruba country, but militarily very weak. Like the Ijebu, their first reaction was to take advantage of the crisis in the Yoruba country, in their own case not so much for trade as for agriculture and war. They welcomed the Oyo refugees seeking land on which to settle. They hoped to control them, partly as mercenary soldiers in their rivalry with the Owu and the Ijesha, even more as a source of cheap labour on their farms. They used the Oyo warriors in destroying Owu and later joined them in destroying the Egba towns and in founding Ibadan, only to discover that the Oyo and not themselves were in control of Ibadan. They gave the refugees land on which to settle on terms of tenancy involving heavy payments in services of different kinds, clearing and cultivating farms, building and roofing houses. Before long, the Ife began to realize that their new tenants would be difficult to control

[1] Gollmer to Straith, Badagry 25 Oct. 1850 (C.M.S. CA2/043).
[2] Dunglas (1949a). Dunglas estimates Dahomey losses at Aro at more than 3,000 killed, a larger number wounded, not counting hundreds captured.

especially when they enjoyed the support of Ibadan. This intractable problem worried one Oni after another right down to this century. In the late 1840's, the Oni Adegunle Abeweila attempted to solve the problem by creating a separate township at Modakeke just outside Ile-Ife for the bulk of the unassimilated settlers. But this only created a centre for them. By 1852 they were strong enough to risk war with Ife and the Oni had for a while to evacuate to Isoya. Ibadan intervened, and negotiated terms of settlement in 1854.[1]

In spite of all these conflicts, and apart from wars in Ekiti, an uneasy peace reigned in the Yoruba country in the late 1850's. Everybody was tired of the crisis. The question was how to achieve and preserve peace. Ibadan's power was becoming dominant. In a sense, this isolated her as the other states began to come closer and to watch the growing power with suspicion. On the other hand the Ibadan were playing their hand very skilfully. They had no intention of reducing their power but they began a diplomatic offensive to break their isolation in the name of uniting the Old Oyo empire against the common enemy, the Fulani at Ilorin. They argued that they alone had for too long borne the burden of resisting Ilorin, that all the Yoruba should stop their fratricidal wars and join them. This met with little response outside the Oyo-speaking areas; but when they went to relieve Ottun in 1854 (then besieged by Ilorin) and to punish Ikoro, Ara and Ijero for allying with Ilorin, they had the support of most of the Oyo excepting Ijaye and the areas controlled by the Are. In this way Ibadan scored two important diplomatic victories.

First, while continuing to wield all the power, Ibadan was making a show of acknowledging the suzerainty of the Alafin and of urging all Oyo states to do the same. Thus, it succeeded in winning over the traditional forces of the Alafin to support its military dominance.[2] Secondly, it was gradually isolating the Are of Ijaye who saw this new policy as only a conspiracy

[1] Johnson, pp. 230–3; Townsend to Venn, 29 July 1852 (C.M.S. CA2/o85); Hinderer, 'Journal of a Missionary Journey, Aug.–Sept. 1858' (including visits to Ife, Modakeke and Isoya) (C.M.S. CA2/o49).
[2] Hinderer to Venn, 26 Oct. 1855 (C.M.S. CA2/o49).

73

against him. Ibadan argued that nothing was further from its intention. That in fact it wished to end Ijaye's isolation by getting the Are to recognize the Alafin as everybody else had done. But the terms of settlement Ibadan suggested involved the Are giving up at least part of the area he controlled to pay tribute to the Alafin. In the circumstances, the Are proceeded to improve the defences of Ijaye. In January 1855 he showed missionaries round the new extensions in the town wall which now enclosed 'a considerable extent of land to the old town, surmounting hills crossing rivers and valleys'.[1] He complained of traps laid for him by the Oyo and Ibadan people. 'If they wish for war let them tell it openly, I am ready to fight. These are the people who speak of peace but secretly they injure us.'[2] There were reports of an arms race, and premonitions of a bloody war.[3] But Ibadan's diplomatic manœuvres were such that Kurunmi was obliged to bide his time. In November 1855 Ibadan convened a peace conference of all the Oyo states, not at Oyo, but significantly at Ibadan. The Alafin was represented and he sent a present of a cow to the delegates. The Are refused to attend in person, but he agreed to make peace and he sent representatives. A general peace was proclaimed not only among the Oyo states, but also with other Yoruba states like the Egba, Ijebu and Ife.[4]

It began to appear therefore that if only the Are could be controlled, the Oyo-Ibadan alliance would restore peace to northern Yoruba and would be able to extend it to the rest of the country. It seemed that Atiba's policy of patience was bearing fruit. He became more optimistic as he proclaimed the good tidings that hitherto 'no one knew who was king but now there is only one king in Yoruba'.[5] And although he began to lean more towards Ibadan, he avoided any open clash with Ijaye and he maintained diplomatic relations with other

---

[1] Mann, Journal, 17 Jan. 1855 (C.M.S. CA2/066).   [2] *Ibid.*

[3] Gollmer, Journal, 2 Feb. 1855, Lagos (C.M.S. CA2/043).

[4] Barber, a Yoruba catechist, to Hinderer, 25 Nov. 1855, enclosed in Hinderer to Venn, 4 Dec. 1855 (C.M.S. CA2/049). Also Mann, Journal, Dec. 1855 (C.M.S. CA2/066).

[5] Hinderer, Journal, 30 May 1856 (C.M.S. CA2/049).

parts of the Yoruba country. The increasing splendour of the annual King's Festival at Oyo reflected Atiba's growing optimism. He made elaborate preparations for the festival of 15 February–1 March 1858, celebrating it as the *Bebe*, a ceremony which only monarchs with long prosperous reigns ever attempted to stage as few are known to have long survived it.[1]

[1] Johnson, pp. 329–30; Meakin, Journal, 15 Feb.–1 March 1858 (C.M.S. CA2/069). For a description of the King's Festival in 1856, see Hinderer, Journal, 26 Jan. 1856 (C.M.S. CA2/049).

III

THE OUTBREAK OF WAR:
c. 1858–MARCH 1860

Behind the complacency of the *Bebe* Festival, there must have
been, besides the Are of Ijaye, one other problem worrying
Atiba: the problem of the succession. At Old Oyo, the kingship rotated in different segments of the ruling lineage. When
a monarch died, his eldest son and his leading officials who
had shared office with him died with him. His other children
usually retired into exile to seek adventure and await their
turn. The kingmakers, interpreting the Ifa Oracle, then decided which of the eligible men of the next segment of the ruling lineage should be appointed. In the crisis in which the old
capital was abandoned, following the death of Alafin Oluewu
in war, none of these formalities was observed. Atiba assumed
the monarchy, decided on the site of the new capital which he
had seized from its founder Oja. It then became the dilemma
of the revolutionary prince turned conservative king to decide
in his old age how to order the succession. If tradition was to
be followed, his Crown Prince Adelu who had been a close
companion and confidant would die with him. The succession
would then be disputed between claimants from the Old Oyo
ruling lineage and the children of Oja who laid claims at least
to the headship of the town their father had founded, and there
would be no traditional kingmakers to resolve the dispute. The
position Atiba had carefully and patiently built up for the
monarchy would then be imperilled. He therefore decided
that, contrary to tradition, Adelu should succeed him. And
he got the rulers of Ibadan to support him in this decision.[1]

---

[1] Johnson implies there was a formal act to change the law of inheritance. In
the absence of supporting evidence, this must be regarded as no more than
Johnson's effort to explain the unusual succession of Adelu. Hinderer, talking
about the causes of the war, said the Bale of Ibadan supported Adelu because

Atiba died on 18 April 1859. For three days all was quiet and tense while emissaries went round the different states. Meanwhile the funeral ceremonies began. The senior and the favourite wives and the chief of the king's bodyguard were the first to accompany the deceased king on his journey. Others were preparing to follow. Then the party opposed to Adelu's succession, led by the Ashipa (a descendant of Oja) and the Are of Ijaye began to demand that Adelu should himself accompany his father as tradition demanded. On 21 April it looked as if civil war might break out between supporters of both groups, but Ibadan intervened and the funeral ceremonies proceeded. At the end of three weeks, on 7 May, Adelu was crowned at a private ceremony.[1] As long as Adelu had the support of Ibadan, the Are of Ijaye was unable to prevent his accession. But the Are refused to recognize him as king. Thus the old crisis was resumed only in an aggravated form. Between the Are and Atiba there had been mutual respect. They had seen so much together. And although the Are was intransigent, Atiba had been patient and diplomatic. Adelu was in time to become as renowned a diplomat as his father; but at the start of his reign his grasp of affairs was less than sure. He was described in 1863 by one of his leading officials as 'young and headstrong; when he was vexed there was no doing anything with him'. A missionary added that he 'had nothing of the kind and condescending manner of his late father and predecessor'.[2] He precipitated the crisis his father had been staving off for years.[3]

'as many of the Yoruba laws were broken through the late wars and we had come to a new time, he did not see why the law concerning a successor should not be broken too' (Hinderer to Venn, 25 April 1860. C.M.S. CA2/049). Although Islam and the upheavals of the wars were modifying the nature of the Yoruba family, the laws of inheritance remained unchanged. In any case, succession to chieftaincies and public offices, where different groups fought to preserve their traditional rights, admitted change more slowly than private inheritance. Adelu was succeeded not by his son but by one of his brothers.

[1] Meakin, Journal, 19, 20, 21 April and 7 May 1859 (C.M.S. CA2/069). Also Reid to Taylor, 23 May 1859 (S.B.C.).

[2] Hinderer to Venn, 18 Aug. 1863, quoting Kudefu. Also 29 Sept. 1863 (C.M.S. CA2/049).

[3] A possible explanation of Adelu's precipitate action is given by Meakin:

The incidents that sparked off the war arose out of the attempt of the new Alafin to contest the Are's claim to supremacy over the provinces west of the upper Ogun. With a combination of conciliation and force the two rulers were using every opportunity to test their strength in the area, with the result that the different towns and villages began to take sides, some for the Are, others for the Alafin.[1] The town of Shaki was for the Alafin and when towards the end of 1859 a contingent from Ijaye attempted to enforce the will of the Are they were overwhelmed, some 90 of the troops being made prisoners. Ibadan intervened and the prisoners were returned. Early in January 1860 another affray occurred at Okeho. The town had formerly paid tribute to Ijaye, but the chief was now willing to pay tribute to the Alafin. But there was a strong party led by a formidable rich widow, perhaps the Are's mother-in-law, who were determined to remain loyal to Ijaye. The chief invited the Alafin to send troops to enforce his will. They were however met by Ijaye troops who, after an initial repulse, succeeded in capturing some 80 prisoners, including a number of market women travelling under protection of the soldiers. Once again, Ibadan intervened to get Ijaye to return the prisoners, but the Are refused. He offered to accept ransom but at a fairly steep rate. Thrice Ibadan sent delegations to the Are. Each time their demand was rejected with increasing humiliation. The last time, the Are in a fit of temper called the

the upsurge of loyalty to Atiba in his last years had visibly increased the tribute coming to Oyo from the Upper Ogun; Adelu, anxious to conciliate the people and chiefs of Oyo, had therefore been able to abolish what Meakin called 'several disagreeable taxes etc. which the people were unwilling to submit to'; a revival of the Are's hold on the Upper Ogun would at once diminish the tribute and necessitate new taxes at Oyo and undermine Adelu's position there (Meakin to Major Straith, 24 Aug. 1859, and to the Secretaries, 15 May 1860, C.M.S. CA2/069).

[1] A reliable guide to the influence of the Are in the Upper Ogun was the reaction of the chiefs there to his officials who sometimes accompanied the missionaries on tour. In 1854, Townsend reported that while at Okeho the chiefs prostrated, at Saki they took little notice of him. A leading chief, he said, 'told me that the Are had no influence at Shaki. . . That they were strong enough to defend themselves from their enemies and therefore independent, but they rendered service to Atiba as the rightful king of the country' (Townsend, Journal, 11 and 14 Jan. 1854. C.M.S. CA2/085).

Ibadan chiefs names and insulted the Ogboni staff which the deputation carried as symbol of authority. It would appear that the Are had decided that war was inevitable and that it was time to provoke it.[1]

When the crisis first began, leading chiefs at Oyo were critical of the action of the Alafin on the grounds partly that they had not been consulted, and partly also that he was too hasty in dealing with the stubborn old war lord at Ijaye.[2] But the intransigence of the Are began to win support for the Alafin. The persistence with which the Ibadan demanded the return of the prisoners and the final insult to their chiefs and staff of authority left them with little alternative but to prepare for war.

Yet the decision to fight Ijaye was a difficult one to take. The rivalry between Ibadan and Ijaye had not altered the fact that there was a very close blood relationship between individuals and lineages in the two places. In the migration southwards, some segments of the same lineage had settled in Ijaye, others in Ibadan. They came together on family occasions like important funerals and festivals. They all bore the same facial marks and in the event of war would not be able to distinguish one from the other on the battlefield. As the Osi, the third leading war chief, put it at a public meeting, he had no less than 120 close relatives at Ijaye; was he then to go and fight

[1] This account is based largely on the C.M.S. which derived principally from Meakin, Journal, 17 Jan. 1860 (C.M.S. CA2/069). Reid to Taylor, 25 Jan. 1860 (S.B.C.) agrees substantially with this. Also Mann to Venn, 18 June 1860 (C.M.S. CA2/066), Hinderer to Venn, 19 March and 26 April 1860 (C.M.S. CA2/049). The suggestion that the rich widow was the Are's mother-in-law comes from Burton (1863), p. 264. Johnson agrees with this account but for two important details. First, he makes Ijanna probably a typographical error for Iganna near Okeho, and not Okeho the home of the rich widow. Secondly, he explains the intervention of Adelu by his desire, not to collect tribute, but to collect the property of a rich widow who dies intestate, a foreign legal concept. In spite of the wealth of circumstantial evidence in Johnson—the rich widow's name was Abu and so on—I have preferred the missionary accounts because while arguing on the rights and wrongs of the combatants they were agreed on these facts and they must have taken some trouble to check them. Both Meakin and Reid were resident at Oyo at the time.

[2] Reid to Taylor, 25 Jan. 1860. Contrast Reid to Taylor, 20 March 1860 (S.B.C.).

them?[1] Opinion in Ibadan was sharply divided. The Bale, an old bed-ridden man, as well as Balogun Ibikunle, the commander-in-chief and effective head of the town, were for patience. The Are was an old man, they pleaded. His age, his past services as a general demanded respect. His death which could not be long delayed would resolve the conflict. The younger war chiefs, however, led by Chief Ogunmola the Otun Balogun, next in rank to the Balogun and traditionally his rival, were for war.[2] The intransigence of the Are merely strengthened their hand. They began to organize public opinion to put pressure on the Balogun. They tied a crow to his house implying he was a coward if he refused to sanction war.[3] The chiefs held meeting after meeting, some public, others private, to discuss the issue of war or peace. In the end the Balogun yielded, it was said, partly to avoid civil strife in Ibadan and partly also because he still believed that war preparations at Ibadan might induce the Are to come round and negotiate.

General mobilization was ordered. The usual ceremonies and sacrifices were undertaken, including a human sacrifice on 10 March to induce good fortune from Oranyan, the founder of Old Oyo.[4] Embassies began to go round neighbouring states to effect a diplomatic isolation of Ijaye. By the third week of February, the roads between Ibadan and Ijaye were watched and it was no longer safe for individual traders or farmers to move freely. The Baptist missionaries at Ijaye, fearing for the safety of J. C. Vaughan, a Liberian member of their Church who lived on his farm some 20 miles south of Ijaye, sent a young American missionary R. H. Stone and another Liberian, Russell, to rescue him. They reached his farm to discover he had left by another route. On their way back

---

[1] Hinderer to Venn, 19 March 1860 (C.M.S. CA2/049).
[2] *Ibid.* Also Johnson, p. 333.   [3] Johnson, p. 333.
[4] Hinderer to Venn, 19 March 1860 (C.M.S. CA2/049). Details of the sacrifice will be found in Anna Hinderer, pp. 212–13. 'A man of about 25 or 30. In the day he was paraded through the market. . . He looked as proud as possible of the honours that awaited him. From being a poor slave, on that day he was all but worshipped.'

they were sighted by a detachment of Ibadan troops, who, according to Stone, numbered about 1,000 and included Nupe mercenaries. They were captured and sent to Ibadan. There, the Balogun released them and sent them to the C.M.S. missionary, David Hinderer, who was away at Abeokuta. They stayed a few days with the catechist Henry Johnson, and returned through Iwo to Oyo back to Ijaye, after nine days of adventure.[1] On 26 March, an Ibadan contingent under the command of Ajayi Ogboriefon arrived at Oyo to guard the capital.[2] Later it established itself at a camp at Ilora.

The neighbouring states watched these proceedings closely but hesitated to take any decisive steps. Those most immediately concerned were the Egba. For them, the growing conflict went beyond the Ijaye-Ibadan rivalry. It was known all that dry season of early 1860 that Dahomey was preparing a new invasion of Abeokuta. The invading army was reported already on the way. It was also known that Dahomey emissaries had been seeking allies in different Yoruba states, at Ijaye, Ibadan, Oyo and even Ilorin. The Egba were therefore already mobilized in preparing to resist the invasion. As part of the measures the British residents at Abeokuta, led by Henry Townsend, the Anglican missionary, appealed to the British Consul at Lagos for aid. The Consul helped to recruit some 300 Egba in Lagos, mostly repatriates from Sierra Leone, for the defence of Abeokuta. He also encouraged merchants to sell ammunition to the Egba. He himself sent 20 barrels of gunpowder, 2 cwts of lead and 18 iron shots from the consular arsenal, besides 30 rounds of shot and cartridge obtained from the anti-slavery naval squadron. Before the middle of March, however, the fears of an immediate invasion passed away. The Dahomey troops, it was reported, had returned home not finding the omens favourable.[3] The Egba could therefore turn their attention to the crisis on their northern border.

[1] R. H. Stone to Taylor, 22 Feb. (from Ibadan), 26 March 1860; Reid to Taylor, 20 March 1860 (S.B.C.). Also Stone.

[2] Meakin, Journal entry for 26 March 1860 (C.M.S. CA2/049).

[3] Biobaku, pp. 64–5; British residents to Consul Brand, 19 Feb. 1860 (PP 1860 LXIV).

The Egba had received a deputation from Ibadan asking them either to mediate in the dispute or to ally with Ibadan or at least to remain neutral. They had sent emissaries of their own to Ijaye in an attempt to mediate but had found the Are implacable. They had sent a friendly message back to Ibadan reporting their failure at Ijaye without committing themselves as to their future action.[1] Now that Ibadan had decided on war, Ijaye appealed to the Egba for support pointing out that if Ijaye fell Ibadan would move next on Abeokuta. The Egba now had to make up their minds. What weighed most heavily with them was the 'intriguing correspondence' between Dahomey and Ibadan and Oyo, the possibility of a coalition between them, perhaps with Ijebu assistance, to destroy Abeokuta. They were impressed by the Are's argument that the real objective of Ibadan was probably Abeokuta, and that they had attacked Ijaye first only to clear the way. Or, as it was expressed at Abeokuta, that Ogunmola the Otun of Ibadan had threatened to 'shave the occiput once he had finished shaving the crown of the head.' Besides this genuine fear, hatred of Ibadan lingered on at Abeokuta. It was Ibadan that had taken the lead in destroying Egba towns and villages in the 1820's. The Egba had by no means forgotten their old homesteads where the ashes of their fathers lay in farms now belonging to Ibadan.[2] Indeed, some Egba had gone back to farm in

---

[1] This early Ibadan embassy is not mentioned in contemporary records, but it probably took place. *Iwe Irohin*, 24 March, mentions an Egba embassy to Ibadan, presumably before 11 March, 'to try to reconcile both parties'. Johnson's claim (p. 334), accepted by Ajisafe, p. 67, that Ogunmola forestalled the Ijaye envoy and got the Egba to 'take an oath of friendship and neutrality with Ibadan', seems to indicate strong oral tradition at Ibadan but it is not supported by the written evidence. Indeed, it seems likely that Johnson here transfers the story of alleged Egba perfidy at the Batedo War of 1844 to the Ijaye War. Hinderer to Venn, 25 April 1860, says 'What Egba does not know that the Egbas have *on a former occasion* received large presents from *the late* Basorun of Ibadan that they may help him to war Ijaye and when it came to the war at that time, the Egbas helped Ijaye instead.' (C.M.S. CA2/049.) (my italics). This tradition referred to the time of Basorun Oluyole, not Basorun Ogunmola.

[2] For Egba motivation in the war, see Townsend for the Alake to Consul Brand, 30 April 1860 (PP 1860 LXIV); *Iwe Irohin*, 24 March 1860; Townsend to Venn, 4 Oct. 1860 (C.M.S. CA2/085); Thomas King to Venn, 6 May 1860

little hamlets on the section of the land not yet effectively occupied by Ibadan. Two such settlements at Ido and Ilugun were destroyed by Ibadan troops early in March as they moved to cross the Ogun to cut off supplies of arms from the Badagry and Porto Novo markets to Ijaye.[1] There was a growing demand that the destruction of these hamlets at the critical time when the Egba were expecting a Dahomey invasion should be used as a *casus belli* to declare war on Ibadan. It is true Ijaye also stood on land formerly cultivated by the Egba, and there was no great love for Ijaye on this account, but there was less hatred. Alliance with Ibadan was out of the question. Neutrality was unwise. Alliance with Ijaye might well prove the first step in the recovery of the old Egba country. The Egba were drifting to war but they moved cautiously, and (with their cumbrous constitution) very slowly.

When a fresh deputation came from Ibadan on 11 March apologizing for the destruction of Ido and Ilugun, and returning four of the 16 prisoners caught in Ibadan's opening manœuvres, the Egba delayed five days while these matters were actively discussed in secret enclaves of the Ogboni and war councils of the different wards and sections of the town. On 15 March a public meeting was held where it was decided to take a firmer line with Ibadan, short of declaring war. The Ibadan envoys were to report that the Egba were for peace, but that Ibadan was already guilty of aggression and if Ibadan did not stop all hostilities forthwith, the Egba would be forced to declare war on the side of Ijaye. This amounted to an ultimatum and Ibadan of course rejected it. Five days later, at a mammoth public meeting attended by an estimated 8,000,

---

(C.M.S. CA2/061). Also the Petition of Egba Christians to the British Government, Nov. 1861 (M.M.S.) explaining among other things why they went to war: 'Is it not good for any one to be anxious to recover his father's land that [he] had been deprived of for so many years when there is chance to regain it? Thinking there is no injustice in recovering our father's land, we therefore join with our king.'

[1] Hinderer to Venn, 25 April 1860 (C.M.S. CA2/049), accepted these facts but argued that Ibadan had, and could have had, no designs on Abeokuta, on the grounds that Ibadan knew that if Dahomey cleared Abeokuta out of the way it would itself be in danger.

'all of male sex able to bear arms', the sins of Ibadan against the Egba were publicly reviewed in order to prepare people's minds for war, and then general mobilization was ordered. The gates and trade routes were formally declared closed to stop young men trying to avoid going to war.[1] When the British Consul at Lagos heard of this and sent a naval officer Lieutenant Lodder and two Egba merchants, Messrs Turner and Robbins, to try to mediate and stop the war, the Egba sent them on to Ibadan to discover for themselves that war had already broken out.

At Ijaye, general mobilization had been ordered in the middle of February. But the Are had first to grapple with an unexpected constitutional problem. The chiefs had watched him drift into war. In his usual authoritarian way he had hardly consulted either the Areagoro, the civil chief next in rank to him or the Balogun, his leading military chief. But the war that was breaking out was not one man's affair. The Are had kept a strict monopoly over the importation of arms and ammunition. Now the Ibadan watched the roads to the coast. Early in March the Areagoro led the chiefs to barricade the main gates, threatening to surrender them to Ibadan unless the Are made some concessions. The Are placated them with gifts and promises and the war preparations went ahead.[2] On 9 March the resident missionaries watched him review his troops: 'Some were armed with swords and shields, some with bows and arrows, others with great cross bows, but the greater part had muskets. There was no artillery'.[3] In that state of preparedness, both sides waited, probably for the new moon, probably also for the other side to make the first move.

Meanwhile, diplomatic negotiations went on in the search for more allies. In particular, the Are was negotiating not only with the Egba but also with Ilorin and Ijebu. To start with, the Ijebu were non-committal. Messengers from Ilorin were however reported at Ijaye on 6 April, promising aid after the

---

[1] *Iwe Irohin*, 24 March 1860. See also the Jones Report, Appendix for a description of a similar 'Oro' meeting in June 1861.
[2] Stone, pp. 170–1.   [3] *Ibid.* p. 172.

Ramadan fast.[1] The Ibadan did not seek formal alliances as such: they hoped for support from bands of mercenaries from Benin, Nupe and Borgu, these last under a prince who believed he lost his bid for the throne following the Are's intervention on the other side.[2]

[1] Phillips to Taylor, 6 and 13 April 1860 (S.B.C.); Reid to Taylor, 10 April 1860, quoting the Baptist Agent at Ogbomosho (S.B.C.).

[2] Stone, p. 141; Reid to Taylor, 8 April 1861 (S.B.C.).

IV

THE FIRST PHASE: MARCH–NOVEMBER 1860

Ibadan moved first. Towards the end of March, Ogunmola, 'in his scarlet robe and [riding] a fine horse', led the bulk of the Ibadan army (estimated at over 60,000[1]) towards Ijaye. They were sighted on the way by some Ijaye troops and there occurred a brief skirmish at Apata Ika, midway between Ibadan and Ijaye. The Ijaye troops soon withdrew as the Are had decided to wait on the defensive and use Ijaye as his base.[2] The Ibadan army moved on and pitched their camp at Olorisaoko, some seven miles from Ijaye. There they were later joined by Balogun Ibikunle and the veterans.[3]

The camp was of the nature of a new town, several mud huts quickly thrown up with thatched roofs. Shaded trees were selected for look-outs and hunter scouts were posted around. Small detachments of troops watched the main lines of communication. As they dug themselves in at the camp, a market developed nearby, and, as much as possible, the social life of a town was maintained. The main amusements were the war drummers and the singers attached to the leading war lords, who constantly echoed familiar songs in praise of their lords, abused their opponents, praised valour and threatened their adversaries. The leading chiefs had wives to look

---

[1] Phillips to Taylor, 23 May 1860, said '60,000–70,000' (S.B.C.). Stone, p. 141, says 'about 100,000'.

[2] Johnson, p. 336.

[3] Johnson, p. 336, says Ogunmola waited for Balogun Ibikunle four miles from Ibadan and that they both marched out together. But Phillips to Taylor, 10 April 1860, said that the Ibadan army encamped near Ijaye was 'under Ogunmola'. Similarly, oral tradition at Olorisaoko associates the founding of the war camp with the name of Ogunmola, not with Ibikunle. Thus, Ogunmola's overwhelming personality notwithstanding, it is hard to believe that the Balogun and the Ottun arrived at Olorisaoko at the same time.

after them and the other soldiers also often received guests from the town. The troops were organized in little bands under the war lords of the different lineages. These groups lived and fed together, and fought under their leaders whose titles indicated their positions in the battle formation.[1] One of the major war efforts was to supply provisions for the people in the camp. This is one reason why wars usually began towards the end of the dry season when maize and yam crops would soon be ready for reaping. The army could then live off the farms. Where a long siege was expected, farms were cultivated round the camp. At Ibadan itself, the Iyalode, head of the women chiefs, and the civil line of chiefs organized supplies from the Ibadan farms and markets.

After a fortnight of organization, culminating, it was said, in five days of feasting, Ibadan troops began to approach Ijaye. On the night of 10 April, Ijaye moved out some troops to catch the Ibadan forces unawares and engage them in battle very early on the morrow. However, they found the Ibadan well prepared, having crossed the Ose and come quite close to Ijaye. Battle raged for some hours before the Ijaye decided to withdraw, claiming to have killed 60 of the Ibadan and captured 80.[2]

Following this preliminary engagement, the first major battle of the war came two weeks later on 26 April when both sides marched out in full battle array.

As the Ibadan were reported on the march, the Ijaye (estimated at over 30,000[3]) moved out similarly in battle formation. The Are set his staff under a cotton tree at Alore on a hill

---

[1] Johnson, pp. 131–7; cf. Biobaku, p. 22, on the Egba army: 'An Ologun chief commanded a force which he raised himself from among his kinsmen and townsfolk and which was swollen by his household or domestic slaves. The loyalty of such a force was his; he could dispose of such a force as he chose in private forays or in the service of the Egba. In theory, all able-bodied men were liable for war service, but enlistments were in the forces of the great Ologun of one's township.' See also the Jones Report, Appendix.

[2] Stone to Taylor, 11 April 1860 (S.B.C.). Also Stone, p. 172; Phillips to Taylor, 13 April 1860; Phillips to Brother Priest, 23 May 1860 (S.B.C.).

[3] Stone to Taylor, 11 April 1860, says 'not much less than 40,000. . . Many of the soldiers were dressed gaily and all were armed with swords, shields, bows, arrows, daggers, muskets' (S.B.C.).

just outside the walls, and his Balogun led the army to the plain below. Although bows and arrows still featured in the Ibadan army, they had proportionately more muskets than the Ijaye. They too had no artillery. They were, however, more numerous and on the whole their generals were younger men exercised constantly in recent wars against Ilorin, whereas the Ijaye leaders tended to be older men bred in the military tactics of the last days of Old Oyo.

The two armies met on the banks of the Ose, 'a little over a mile from the Ijaye walls'. For identification, the Ibadan troops wore blades of grass in their caps. Each side tried to provoke the other to cross the brook. Probably as a sign of greater discipline on the Ibadan side, they won the battle of nerves. Some young Ijaye warriors itching for battle tried to rush a ford and they were dreadfully punished. The Ijaye then, as if retreating, drew back and allowed Ibadan to cross the brook in pursuit. Then the Ijaye made a stand in Are's own farms and battle went on for over six hours with comparatively heavy losses on both sides before darkness intervened.[1]

Ijaye claimed to have won the battle of Ose. The Ibadan believed, however, that the Ijaye had been shaken, the Are having barely escaped capture. They pressed the advantage, hoping to wear the Ijaye out or exhaust their ammunition before their allies came to their aid, or at any rate, if possible, before the heavy rains started. Within a fortnight, three major battles were fought on the same site, each one harder than the previous one.[2] At the end of the battles, the Ijaye looked far from worn out although there were rumours of the stock of ammunition getting low. The expected allies were slow in coming. True, the Ilorin began to intervene as promised after the Ramadan fast, but only fitfully. They came in little mounted detachments to raid Oyo farms. Once, in the middle of May, they raided Koso, a sacred grove on the outskirts of the town, where they killed three of the official guards and kidnapped

[1] Phillips to Brother Priest, 23 May 1860 (S.B.C.). This seems to be the battle described in Johnson, p. 338.

[2] 30 April, 5 May, 10 May (Phillips to Taylor, 22 May 1860. S.B.C.).

seven.[1] These raids failed to create the necessary diversion from the main theatre of war. And when the Alafin protested at the raid on Koso, the Emir of Ilorin professed himself neutral in the war, blaming the raids on irresponsible war chiefs acting without authority.[2] It therefore began to look as if a quick decision would be unlikely. Ijaye began to avoid pitched battles, but Ibadan kept up the pressure, raiding into Ijaye farms and cutting down the forests Ijaye had deliberately left to shelter the town walls.[3] A Baptist missionary at Ijaye expressed the opinion that 'Nothing could have saved [Ijaye] many days longer when the scarlet cloaks of Abeokutan horsemen appeared on the hill just outside the town'.[4] The main army estimated at about 20,000 finally arrived on 19 May.

The Egba were led by Chief Somoye (the Basorun) as the civil authority in charge of policy, and Chief Anoba as the Balogun in charge of the conduct of the war.[5] This division of authority at the battle front presented difficulties both in the planning of the Egba campaigns and in co-ordinating their plans with those of their Ijaye allies. There was constant suspicion that the Egba aimed at more than just giving military assistance to a beleagured neighbour. The first of their disagreements with Ijaye came quite early. The Are had expected them to camp within the walls of Ijaye with the probable implication that the Egba command would be fully integrated with his own. The Egba, however, preferred a greater measure of independent action. They chose to camp outside the main walls.[6]

The Egba built their huts and fortifications like the Iba-

[1] Reid to Taylor, 17 May 1860 (S.B.C.).
[2] Reid to Poindexter, 31 Aug. 1860 (S.B.C.).
[3] Reid to Taylor, 17 May 1860 (S.B.C.).   [4] Stone, p. 175.
[5] Johnson says Anoba was in charge, but all the missionaries believed that the Basorun was in charge because it was he who conducted all negotiations with them. For example, Stone, p. 175, says the Egba forces were under the Basorun; Mann to Venn, no date, probably Jan. 1861, says the Basorun came to ask him for a grant towards the upkeep of the Egba troops (C.M.S. CA2/066).
[6] Johnson, p. 339. Losi, p. 73, apparently quoting the Egba version of the story says it was the Are who compelled the Egba to camp outside the walls to prevent their kidnapping Ijaye people.

dan's. They were similarly armed except that it appears they had a small cannon, one of those they had acquired for the defence of Abeokuta. Their experience in war had however been very different from the Ibadan's. Their greatest military exercise had been in resisting the Dahomey attack on Abeokuta. It had been a defensive war fought from above or just below the embattled walls of the town. When, following the Dahomey war, the Egba had taken the offensive against smaller towns, they had relied on wearing out their opponents through long sieges. They were not used to the manœuvres and pitched battles the Ibadan had developed in their recent wars. For two weeks the Egba organized their camp and built their stockades and it appeared as if they would fall in line with the Are's policy of avoiding pitched battles for the meantime. But they were anxious to fight before the beginning of the rainy season, and the Ibadan, who had not seen the Egba at war for a long time and were anxious to study their tactics, had no difficulty in provoking them to take the initiative.

The allies marched out on 4 June, and their plans soon collapsed because of their mutual suspicion and divided counsels. Each partner blamed the other for the ensuing disaster and it is now difficult to reconstruct the events of the battle.[1] They crossed the Ose in perfect order and approached the Ibadan camp at Olorisaoko; Egba young men were in the van, the main Egba army under Anoba on the right, the main Ijaye army on the left, and the Are leading the veterans at the rear. The plan, it seems, was that the van should approach the Ibadan and draw them out to fight on the left wing while Anoba should lead the Egba to outflank them on the right and attack them from the rear. Unknown to the allies, the Ibadan had prepared themselves in a long line stretching for miles on the banks of a brook, since called Fejeboju[2] under cover of tall grass. The Egba van came up against them unexpectedly

---

[1] Johnson, pp. 340–1; King to Venn, Abeokuta, 6 June 1860 (C.M.S. CA2/061); Reid to Taylor, 17 June 1860 (S.B.C.). Stone, pp. 176–8.

[2] 'Fejeboju' means 'washing face with blood'. So much blood was shed on the banks of the brook that for days if you washed with the water you were also washing with blood.

and were thrown into confusion. The Ijaye on the left wing attacked, but could not hold the Ibadan long enough for the Egba to move out to the right. The Ijaye began to retreat and the Ibadan rallied on the Egba on the right wing and it was they who bore the brunt of the battle. They retreated and the Ibadan pursued. They attempted to make a stand at Ajibade. Battle raged fiercely for a while, but the Egba could not hold their ground. The Ibadan, who knew the terrain very well, were able to push the Egba towards the marshes of Alabata where a good many of them perished or were captured. The Egba had to withdraw in confusion. The Are came to their aid and made a heroic stand long enough to cover their retreat. This however created yet more confusion as the Egba could not tell from their facial marks who were Ijaye and who were Ibadan. That night, so a missionary reported, there was gloom in the Egba camp. 'Trumpets were wailing all night calling the names of the missing in the hope that they might be hid in the bush and be directed by the sound to the camp.'[1] No one knows how many were lost, killed or captured. Soon after the battle, 500 to 1,000 Egba slaves were reported on sale in Ibadan markets. A missionary at Abeokuta, himself Egba, said over 1,000 were lost. Egba Christians, in a petitition to the British 18 months later, probably with some exaggeration, put the number at about 2,000.[2]

The defeat at Ajibade did not make it any easier for the allies to work together. The Are had to order a ban on the abusive songs Ijaye women were composing about the military incompetence of their allies.[3] However, it drew the Egba nearer the Ijaye view that the Ibadan were not to be driven home by one or two pitched battles.[4] Similarly, Ibadan drew the conclusion that with the massive Egba intervention, the

---

[1] Stone, p. 178.

[2] Reid to Taylor, 17 June 1860, quoting a private report from Hinderer (S.B.C.); King to Venn, 6 June 1860 (C.M.S. CA2/061); Petition of Egba Christians to the British Government, November 1861 (M.M.S.).

[3] Stone, p. 178.

[4] Hinderer to Venn, 28 Oct. 1860, saying that since 6 June, 'neither the Egbas nor Ijaye could be provoked to accept an open battle' (C.M.S. CA2/049).

war could not end before the heavy rains. Both sides therefore began to settle down for a prolonged siege to last at least till the next dry season when, after the harmattan, the bush could again be burnt and the streams easily forded. Meanwhile, each side planned secondary operations to build up their stocks, to make new allies and to deprive their opponents of the opportunity of receiving supplies, of both food and ammunition.

There were three main strands to the allied plan. First, they wished to encourage the Ijebu and Ilorin to aid them more actively. It was hoped that an Ilorin invasion of the areas under the control of Ibadan would create a useful diversion of Ibadan troops from the main theatre of war. Ilorin was interested. By September, small mounted detachments from Ilorin resumed raiding on Oyo farms.[1] But, as before, they were fitful and ineffective. The Emir continued to negotiate with all sides, including Dahomey,[2] and refused to be wholly committed to an all-out war in a dispute that concerned mostly non-Muslims. The Ijebu were more vital to the allies, both for recruiting mercenaries and for hindering supplies from getting to Ibadan from Benin and from the Ikorodu market. Ibadan was becoming more and more dependent on this latter route and the allies increased their bid to get the Ijebu on their side. Many towns in Ijebu-Remo, led by Kehere the Balogun of Ipara, were on the side of Ibadan;[3] the people of Ijebu-Ode and Ijebu-Igbo expressed sympathy for the allies, but were slow to commit themselves to active military involvement. In June, they were described as neutral but pro-Egba.[4] By August, the Basorun told the missionaries at Ijaye that the Ijebu were coming round,[5] and the missionary at Ibadan reported that they were beginning to raid Ibadan farms.[6] In

[1] Reid to Poindexter, 1 Oct. 1860 (S.B.C.).

[2] Reid to Poindexter, 2 Nov. 1860 (S.B.C.), reported Dahomey envoys numbering 30 people passing from Oyo to Ilorin. In December Ilorin troops were reported to have attacked Ilobu but were recalled on account of a large conflagration at Ilorin. (Hinderer to Venn, 4 Jan. 1861. C.M.S. CA2/049.)

[3] Johnson, p. 338.   [4] Phillips to Taylor, 13 June 1860 (S.B.C.).

[5] Stone to Poindexter, 28 Aug. 1860, in *The Commission* (Journal of the S.B.C.) Dec. 1860.

[6] Hinderer to Venn, 26 Aug. 1860 (C.M.S. CA2/049).

November, they were described as still vacillating, trying to make a profit from both sides.[1] It would appear, however, that by December the Awujale had definitely come round to the side of the allies. His envoys were reported negotiating serious terms for recruiting Benin mercenaries for them.[2] By January 1861, the Ijebu moved in force into Ibadan farms. They captured Apomu and established Oru as a base from which to harass every caravan taking supplies from the coast to Ibadan.[3]

The second strand of the allied plan was to safeguard their communications to the coast. For this purpose the Egba had maintained an important base at Olokemeji under the command of Chief Ogunbona. The route from there to Abeokuta was relatively safe. From Abeokuta to Lagos was also safe, provided the British Consul at Lagos did not interfere. From Olokemeji to Ijaye was however subject to raids by Ibadan troops who had also succeeded in cutting off Ijaye from Porto Novo and Badagry. Then there was the ever-present fear that Dahomey would interfere with these routes on their own or in alliance with Ibadan, and then invade Abeokuta itself. The Egba were trying to exploit this fear in anti-slave trading circles in Lagos to link up Ibadan with Dahomey and secure active British intervention on their own side.

The third strand involved keeping the lines of communication free not only for ammunition but also for food supplies. For this purpose it was vital for the survival of Ijaye whose farms had been neglected or rendered unsafe to keep control of the Upper Ogun districts. Most of the area, with the notable exception of Shaki and the Ibarapa district, was still loyal to the Are who maintained a base at Irawo to protect his interests.[4]

---

[1] Reid to Poindexter, 2 Nov. 1860 (S.B.C.).

[2] Phillips to Taylor, 4 Dec. 1860; Reid to Taylor, 8 Feb. 1861 (S.B.C.).

[3] Johnson, pp. 337-8, 342-4; Hinderer to Venn, 4 Jan. 1861 (C.M.S. CA2/049). One consequence of the Ijebu involvement in the war was that for the first time missionaries could move more easily between Abeokuta and Ijebu Ode. Thomas Champness, a Methodist missionary, took the opportunity, while it lasted, to visit Ijebu Ode, 31 Aug. to 6 Sept. 1861 (Champness to Osborn, 7 Oct. 1861 (M.M.S.), giving details of the journey).

[4] Stone to Taylor, 11 April 1860 (S.B.C.).

The Ibadan plan was to tighten their hold on the inner front around the farms and immediate surroundings of Ijaye. From there they could protect their line of communication with Ijebu Remo and Lagos as well as with Porto Novo and Badagry. Their eastern front was relatively safe as they believed that Ilorin was not sufficiently interested in the fight between non-Muslim states to intervene conscientiously. The one major gap in their scheme of encircling Ijaye was the Upper Ogun districts. It was therefore vital that they should press Ijaye on that front.

All that rainy season from mid June to November, desultory fighting went on, with relatively even honours on both sides, in escorting or in attacking transport caravans.[1] Nevertheless, it was a critical time for both sides. It was critical for Ijaye because with the disposition of forces, its farms and lines of communication were most vulnerable. By the end of June, it was unsafe to sow or reap crops anywhere in Ijaye farms outside the town walls. Oje, a well-known war chief who had negotiated the alliance with the Egba and had taken a prominent part in the fighting at Ose and had become famous in escorting caravans from the coast through Ibadan lines, lost his life trying to protect reapers on his farm.[2] The Ibadan blockade was already causing famine in Ijaye town, especially among women and children.[3] The missionaries, who had made little progress at Ijaye, began to find new opportunities in the situation. First the American Baptists, then the Anglicans, offered to take children into their homes and feed and educate them, and in this way began to fill hitherto empty schools.[4] By

[1] Stone to Poindexter, 28 Aug. 1860, in *The Commission* (S.B.C.), Dec. 1860.

[2] Reid to Poindexter, 31 Aug. 1860 (S.B.C.), said it happened 'a few weeks ago'. He was caught alive. At the camp, he was executed, his hands and feet cut off and burnt. One Samuel Cole, an Egba schoolmaster at Ijaye was captured on the Iseyin road, but was later released (Johnson, pp. 334, 351, 353–4).

[3] To at least one detached observer in Lagos, the fate of the allies already began to appear gloomy. Maser, a C.M.S. missionary wrote: 'It seems Ijaye (without provision) and the Egbas (having no open road from their encampment at Ijaye to Abeokuta) are the worse for a chance of success in the struggle' (Maser to Venn, 13 Aug. 1860. C.M.S. CA2/068).

[4] Phillips to Taylor, 4 Aug. 1860 (S.B.C.). By that date, the Baptists had

July, apart from supplies from Egba farms, the only farms and markets easily accessible to Ijaye were those of the Upper Ogun districts. Ibadan now began to send detachments of troops from their base at Ilora near Oyo, under the command of Latosisa, to strengthen the hands of pro-Alafin groups in the different towns and villages. During the month of August they attempted to acquire a base in the area most loyal to the Are. They chose Iseyin for this purpose and they succeeded in building up a pro-Ibadan party there. But when they sent in troops to occupy the town, they were expelled for their excesses. Ibadan had to send a bigger expedition not only to occupy Iseyin but also to attempt to take control of the Ijaye base at Irawo.[1] Thus troops began to arrive in large numbers in the Upper Ogun districts, but the rains made effective fighting difficult.

It was in this difficulty that danger lay for Ibadan. The main Ijaye army was within the town walls and the Egba were close to the comforts the town could provide. The Ibadan, however, were couped up in their camp on the farms. They dared not evacuate during the rainy season for if they released the pressure on the Ijaye farms, they would lose all the advantage they had gained. Yet the soldiers were becoming bored with insufficient activity and there was danger of indiscipline. There were already reports circulating of junior chiefs going away on unauthorized campaigns of their own and being caught in Ijesha farms when they should be at the war camp. In the enforced inactivity at the camp, there was growing criticism of the conduct of the war and overt suggestions that the war might have ended before the rains if all sections of the camp had exerted their whole energy in the war.[2]

One important result of this was the gradual undermining

gathered 18 children. Finding feeding difficult, they evacuated the first batch on 29 July. Up to 19 Sept., Mann, the Anglican missionary, was critical of this practice (Mann to Venn, 19 Sept. 1860. C.M.S. CA2/o66). But before November, he too had begun to gather children.

[1] Phillips to Taylor, Abeokuta, 9 Aug. 1860; Reid to Poindexter, 1 Oct. 1860; Phillips to Taylor, 5 Nov. 1860 (S.B.C.); Johnson, pp. 346–7.

[2] Reid to Taylor, 2 Nov. 1860 (S.B.C.).

of the authority of Balogun Ibikunle who had entered the war reluctantly and had been anxious to keep the fighting as well as the treatment of prisoners of war as humane as possible.[1] By the end of the rainy season, it was evident that if the morale of the Ibadan troops was to be kept up, the tempo of the war must be stepped up, the fighting had to become more ruthless, and a speedy decision aimed at. This was the policy being advocated by Chief Ogunmola, the Otun.

[1] Johnson, pp. 350–1.

V

THE SECOND PHASE: DECEMBER 1860–FEBRUARY 1862

This new policy of Ibadan first became obvious in the battle for the control of the Upper Ogun which Ogunmola himself decided to command. He prepared the core of the Ibadan army to set out secretly in the first days of December before anyone expected the war to resume. He passed through Ilora and made for Iseyin which he used as base. The Ijaye soon realized that a large Ibadan force was on the way, but they did not know the immediate objective. They therefore concentrated their forces at the defensible site of Iwawun. That suited Ogunmola as what he wanted was just such concentration so that he could face the main Ijaye force in the area and attempt to smash it at once. Assisted by two of Ibadan's greatest generals of the future, Latosisa and Ajayi Ogboriefon, he attacked Iwawun early on 6 December and in a bitter, ruthless struggle he captured it. The Ijaye troops made a determined stand, but they were crushed. Many of the younger generals died fighting. A number, including five of Are's sons, among them Arawole his eldest surviving son, were captured and killed. The town was completely destroyed and the surrounding farms burnt.[1] Thus, in one single battle, the Ijaye hold on that vital district was broken.

Three days later, on 9 December the allies replied by attacking the Ibadan camp, trying to take advantage of Ogunmola's absence. The bush was still thick, thicker than in the Upper Ogun, and the brooks still a little difficult to cross, but the Are was desperate for revenge.

He staked all he had on the effort to take the Ibadan camp

---

[1] Hinderer to Venn, 4 Jan. 1861 (C.M.S. CA2/049); Reid to Taylor, 8 Feb. 1861 (S.B.C.); Johnson, pp. 347–50.

at Olorisaoko by storm that day. He led his own forces side by side with his Egba allies. But Balogun Ibikunle was a match for him and he was foiled of his great chance. It was another hard-fought battle, with heavy losses on both sides. From early dawn to dusk, the allies could not dislodge the Ibadan or capture the camp. The Are was loath to accept defeat, but he was forced to withdraw.[1] Ogunmola hastened back to the camp, leaving enough troops to deal with Ijaye's outposts at Irawo and Awaye. As he went south he spread further destruction, and using different subterfuges like beating the Are's drums to deceive his opponents, he captured as many Ijaye traders as possible.

These two battles marked a turning point in the war. The military defeat, the loss of his sons, the tarnish on his military reputation, all combined to break the indomitable spirit of the Are. In Samuel Johnson's words, 'It was as if he had received his death warrant; he saw clearly that all hopes for Ijaye were now gone, and with a dejected spirit, he was often seen in his house wandering abstractedly and muttering to himself: "Nje emi ni mo jebi oran yi?" (Am I then in the wrong in this matter?)'[2]

The immediate consequence of the battles was the shrinking of much-needed food supplies from the Upper Ogun districts. This meant not only an increasingly desperate famine in Ijaye town, but also greater dependence on the Egba, their suspicious and much-suspected allies. Caravans were still coming through, bringing food, largely awuje beans, from the Egba farms. Most of this went to the soldiers but some got to the town. The Ijaye people had nothing to sell in exchange and many were obliged to put their children in pawn, not only to missionaries for ready cash, but also to Egba soldiers and traders in return for food. The soldiers were not paid. They saw in the predicament of their Ijaye allies a chance to make some money. The Egba soldiers collaborated with the traders in col-

---

[1] Hinderer to Venn, 4 Jan. 1861 (C.M.S. CA2/049); Johnson, pp. 347–50.
[2] Johnson, p. 350.

lecting such pawns and then selling them into slavery at Okeodan or Badagry, an act which drew much criticism from their
friends and enemies alike.[1] This increasing dependence of the
Ijaye on them also meant that the Egba now became the
senior partners in the war, partners whose policies and interests must predominate. This was yet another wound in the
heart of the Are. It was largely Egba troops and Egba resources that now stood between Ibadan and victory. From an
Ijaye–Ibadan war in which the Egba had intervened, it was
becoming an Egba–Ibadan war in which the control of Ijaye
was to be the ultimate prize.[2] In the circumstances, the Egba
redoubled their efforts to win the war.

For two months, while this new situation was developing,
there was little fighting at the main theatre of the war. The
Egba were reverting to their old policy of avoiding pitched
battles and preferring a long siege. To prepare for this, they
embarked on a new diplomatic offensive. As the dry season
commenced, they thought not only of the Ijaye war but also of
a possible Dahomey invasion. Their view of the necessary system of alliances therefore became broader. They needed more
active support from Ijebu Ode and Ijebu Igbo who, at last
realizing the danger of an over-mighty Ibadan, were prepared to commit themselves to full participation in the war.
But that was not enough. To keep Dahomey busy, the Egba
began to think of possible alliance not only with Ashanti on the

---

[1] Mann to Venn, 19 Sept. 1860 (C.M.S. CA2/066); Harrison to Venn,
30 Sept. 1861 (C.M.S. CA2/045); Champness to Osborn, 6 and 31 March
1862 (M.M.S.). Anglican, Methodist and Baptist missionaries at Abeokuta went
in a body to protest to the Alake against Egba selling Ijaye people. The Alake,
reported one of them, 'seemed not well pleased at our meddling in the matter,
entered into a defence of the war, because the Ibadans lived in their (Egbas')
homes. He said it was not the Egba but the Ijaye people who sold Ijayes. I
never saw him exhibit so much energy as when speaking on this subject'
(Wood to Venn, 6 Sept. 1861. C.M.S. CA2/096).

[2] Stone accuses the Basorun of actually undermining the authority of the
Are, giving titles to Ijaye chiefs against his wish, summoning him peremptorily
to a meeting of the Egba Obgoni at the Egba camp, and at least on one
occasion writing a letter to the Alake, referring to 'a great cotton wood tree in
our way and we must cut it down', meaning the Are. Stone, passim.

west, but also with the British on the coast. To what extent the Ashanti project was pursued, we do not know.[1] But we have some details of the British alliance.

The Ijaye war had seriously affected the volume of trade from the interior to the coast. With the Egba closing their gates and the Ijebu becoming more involved in the war, less and less palm-oil, cotton, indigo and other produce was reaching the British traders in Lagos. To make matters worse, because of the pronounced anti-slavery policy of the British and their support for the Egba, Dahomey exerted pressure on Porto Novo to divert their trade away from Lagos towards Whydah where only traders who accepted Dahomey terms were allowed. By December 1860, British trade in Lagos had been reduced to a trickle. And to protect and expand this trade was the primary duty of the British Consul. Having tried and failed to stop the war, he began to consider measures to hasten its end.[2]

First, he attempted a blockade to stop ammunition reaching the combatants. But this was ineffective. Both sides had powerful friends in Lagos whose livelihood depended on trade and who could easily smuggle ammunition through the blockade. And in any case, if the arms did not come through Lagos, they could come through any of several points along the lagoon between Porto Novo and Benin or even beyond. The Consul could not intervene in the interior because he depended essentially on the naval force of the anti-slavery squadron on the coast. He therefore began to consider an attack on Porto Novo[3] which would not only increase the effectiveness of the British blockade but would also be calculated to divert the Porto Novo trade to Lagos.

It was at this stage that the Egba came into the discussions.

[1] Phillips to Taylor, 4 Dec. 1860, that the Egba were trying to get Ashanti to fight Dahomey to create a diversion (S.B.C.).

[2] Biobaku, pp. 66–7.

[3] Cf. the view of an earlier Consul: that the town of Porto Novo 'unlike that of the king of Jaboo (situated 20 miles inland) is on the banks of the Lagoon, having ample depth of water for small class steamers' (Campbell to Malmesbury, 22 March 1859. FO84/1088).

Aided by the British residents at Abeokuta, mostly missionaries, and their friends in Lagos, the Egba had since the rainy season been trying to persuade the Consul that no measures short of a speedy return of peace could succeed in opening up trade in Lagos.[1] They reminded the British of their traditional alliance, that the Egba were the spearhead of British influence and anti-slavery civilization in the interior, and that the best way to end the war quickly was to give substantial military aid to the Egba and to ban ammunition not from Lagos markets which was not possible, but from the Ikorodu market on which the Ibadan largely depended and which could be more easily controlled. Lieutenant-Commander Hand who had been Acting Consul since June 1860 seemed impressed by this argument. But military aid could only come from the West India Regiment in Sierra Leone and would require lengthy negotiations and the co-operation of many different people. These negotiations had already been initiated when Hand was succeeded on 21 December by Henry Grant Foote, the new Consul from San Salvador. While negotiating for military aid for the Egba, Foote attempted the simpler exercise of a naval bombardment of Port Novo on 24 February 1861.[2]

The huts on the foreshore were destroyed, but little came of it. Consul Foote was therefore more convinced that the easiest way to establish British influence in the area was to build up the Egba as a powerful military power, backed up by the naval squadron.[3] He therefore promised the Egba substantial aid as soon as he could obtain men and ammunition from Sierra Leone.

[1] E.g. Petition of three white traders and four missionaries, 13 Oct. 1860, to Consul Hand, asking for military aid for the Egba, enclosed in Hand to Russell, 3 Nov. 1860 (FO84/1115). Also Chief Sokenu, the Seriki Egba, to Samuel Crowther, 1 Feb. 1861, asking Crowther to be more active in securing military aid for Abeokuta (C.M.S. CA3/04).

[2] Biobaku, pp. 66–7; Newbury, pp. 64–5.

[3] 'If the Egba could make themselves masters of the country, the whole of the petty chiefs on the coast would rejoice at their occupation; and certainly the great object we have in view, viz. the abolition of slavery, would be finally secured if our friends the Egbas did extend their possessions to the coast, including Whydah and the other Dahomian slave ports' (Foote to Lord John Russell, 8 May 1861. PP 1862 LXI).

Meanwhile the Ibadan prepared to resume war in earnest. By 8 February they moved into the attack in the new spirit of determination inspired by Chief Ogunmola. During February, March and April, sharp fighting was going on all the time. The battles became more ferocious and much heroism was shown on both sides. A missionary said of a battle in February:

The roar of musketry was so terrific that it was heard here at Abeokuta and thus announced the battle before it ceased.... One long line of wounded, dead and dying issued from both sides during the whole of the fighting, men with blood gushing from bossoms, would walk back firmly, sternly and even proudly to their camp.[1]

Militarily the honours appeared even. The Ibadan could not end the war as speedily as they had hoped.

With the Ijebu now supporting the allies, the Ibadan were hard put to it to escort their ammunition from Ikorodu through Ijebu-Remo.[2] However, since they maintained their pressure on the Ijaye farms and had cut off the food supplies from the Upper Ogun, they had the advantage of the siege. They began to garrison the intervening hills between their main base at Olorisaoko and Ijaye, and thus to confine the battle ground nearer and nearer to Ijaye.[3]

Effects of the war were becoming noticeable in Ibadan. Food was dearer than ever before, dearer, it was said, in the town than at the camp. But it was still readily available because much farming went on undisturbed. What was very scarce was ready cash in the form of cowries because trade had become so restricted. This told severely on visitors, especially

[1] Stone to Poindexter, Abeokuta, 29 April 1861 (S.B.C.); Bickersteth to Osborn, 7 March 1861, said the Egba Christians in the war fought fearlessly 'like men drunk' (Meth). Also Hinderer to Venn, 19 March 1861, said 'there was sharp fighting last week' (C.M.S. CA2/049).

[2] The difficulties may be judged from the account of Hinderer to Venn, 10 March 1861 (C.M.S. CA2/049). He had joined an Ibadan caravan to and from Lagos in search of provisions for his family.

[3] Johnson, pp. 342 and 351, says they actually moved camp from Olorisaoko to Ajibade, and from Ajibade to Alabata. This is not substantiated by the records, and oral tradition at Olorisaoko does not support the idea of a total abandonment any time during the war except perhaps just before the collapse of Ijaye.

missionaries who depended on cowries to buy their provisions.[1] The position at Abeokuta was similar, except that cowries were not so scarce since communication with coastal markets, especially Lagos, was easier than from Ibadan.[2] At Ijaye, however, the war had brought untold suffering. The famine was becoming intolerable. Old people and children who had relations in Ibadan, Abeokuta and other places began to migrate if they could join escorted caravans to cross the battle fronts. Missionaries began to reduce their staff and to evacuate members of their households especially wives and the large number of children they had recently been taking on to board. To facilitate this, the Anglicans at Abeokuta organized an Ijaye Relief Committee to send cowries and provisions to their colleagues in Ijaye and help in the evacuation.[3] Thus it was not in the interest of the allies just to go on resisting the siege. Their only hope lay in finding additional strength to drive the Ibadan home.

Such additional force appeared within the grasp of the Egba when Consul Foote, accompanied by the Rev. Samuel Ajayi Crowther, paid the Alake a visit in April 1861. The Consul expressed regret that the Egba were so preoccupied with the Ijaye war, as he had a more exciting plan to help them increase their power along the coast, especially to defeat Da-

[1] For the privations of the Hinderers at Ibadan see Anna Hinderer. Also Hinderer to Venn, 10 March 1861, 2 Aug. 1861, 25 Sept. 1861 (C.M.S. CA2/049).

[2] This conclusion is based largely on the absence of material. It was not till 7 Jan. 1862 that Champness complains: 'The war is eating up the vitality of the country. Money is scarce and food dear' (to Osborn, M.M.S.). Even then there was still evidence to the contrary, though coloured by partisan desire to show that things were worse on the other side. Cf. Wood to Venn, 6 Jan. 1863: 'Abeokuta notwithstanding the war has been carrying on trade to a large extent and so far from decaying as Ibadan is said to be, Abeokuta appears only to be getting richer' (C.M.S. CA2/096).

[3] Mann to Venn, no date, probably Jan. 1861, also 2 Oct. 1861 (C.M.S. CA2/066). Johnson, p. 344; 'Starvation and consequent mortality at Ijaye was indescribable. Hundreds, nay thousands died in the streets from starvation, whole families perished without any one to bury them. All the livestock had been consumed, the garden, the streets, and the yards were all planted with corn, but the cornstalks were devoured when they could not wait for the corn to develop.'

homey and in this way establish a more permanent peace and keep the trade routes open. 'The Alake made light of his commitments at Ijaye', and assured the Consul that with some help the Ijaye war could soon be ended and the Egba could then concentrate on the anti-Dahomey project. The Consul then promised a British officer and some troops from Sierra Leone to drill the Egba soldiers and teach them to use artillery more effectively. Thus he would help them to win the Ijaye war and prepare them for a great expedition against Dahomey in the next dry season. The Egba army, so trained and British led, would attack Dahomey while the naval squadron supported it with a blockade and bombardments on the coast.[1] The Egba were of course elated, as this was more than they had expected. And they waited anxiously to welcome the promised British officer.[2]

He arrived at Abeokuta on 10 May, a Captain A. T. Jones of the Second West India Regiment. He said he had come to prepare the way for 250 of his men. He examined the defence of Abeokuta and regretted that the Egba had allowed the seven cannon they had to get rusty on the town walls. He harangued the new recruits who were about to be sent to the battle front, telling them he was coming after them to see

[1] Crowther to Venn, 6 May 1861 (C.M.S. CA3/04); Foote to Russell, 8 May 1861 (PP 1862 LXI).

[2] Both the Colonial Office and the Foreign Office were hesitant about the scheme, but they did not press the point. Newcastle warned the Governor of Sierra Leone of the danger in teaching potential enemies how to use artillery. Governor Hill replied that the Egba were traditional friends and would use their knowledge only for defensive purposes (Hill to Newcastle, 29 June 1861. P.R.O. C.O. 267/270). The real reason why the government did not press their objection would seem to be that, without stressing it, they could see two possible advantages in the venture: (a) such an expedition would return with increased knowledge of the interior. It was written into the instructions of Captain Jones that he was to obtain 'all the military information he could as to the resources of that country and the means they may have of action in an offensive war' (Commodore Edmonstone to Captain Jones, 29 April 1861, enclosed in Hill to Russell, 20 June 1861. P.R.O. FO84/1134). (b) The expedition could also become of great political significance. McCoskry at one time advised the Foreign Office that 'A small body of black troops with white officers quartered in Abeokuta would give us influence enough to settle this war without any fighting and prevent the occurrence of others of a similar nature' (McCoskry to Russell, 31 May 1861. P.R.O. FO84/1141).

if they would fight like men or like women. He criticized Hinderer's staying on at Ibadan as an anti-British act.[1] Then he went to inspect the Egba war camps and to survey the field of battle and to watch some fighting at Ijaye. He returned to Abeokuta full of criticism of their conduct of the war and their performance in battle.[2] However, he then left for Lagos to await the arrival of his men and to bring them up, the Alake sending three large canoes down the Ogun to transport them. But the day before he left Abeokuta, Consul Foote had died in Lagos and he arrived to find a trader, William McCoskry, an old enemy of the Egba, as Acting Consul. By then, only ten of the expected troops had arrived. McCoskry countermanded the orders of Captain Jones, explaining later that 'From the report of Capt. Jones who has been at the seat of the war between Abeokuta and Ibadan, I see no probability of the war being terminated by military operations this year'.[3] He ordered the ten soldiers to join the consular guard, the others he expected to return to Sierra Leone. Captain Jones was to go up to the Ibadan camp to try to negotiate a truce. He then addressed a peremptory letter to the Egba to demonstrate their affection for the British cause by giving up the war and returning to their trade. Jones died on his way to Ibadan, and the war dragged on again into the rainy season.

There was some hope of a negotiated peace during that rainy season. For, probably late in June or some time in July, 'the Are who has died so often before is at last dead.'[4] For

---

[1] Wood to Venn, 5 July 1861, 7 Nov. 1861 (C.M.S. CA2/096). Also Petition of the Egba Christians, Nov. 1861 (M.M.S.).

[2] Captain Jones to the officer commanding Second West India Regiment, Sierra Leone, 6 June 1861, enclosed in Governor Hill to Russell, 20 June 1861 (P.R.O. FO84/1134).

[3] McCoskry to Russell, 4 July 1861 (PP 1862 LXI). In his handing over notes to Governor Freeman, McCoskry said he opposed the scheme of strengthening the Egba on the grounds that it would make the British too dependent on them (enclosed in Freeman to Russell, 4 June 1862. P.R.O. FO84/1175). For the Report of Captain Jones, see Appendix.

[4] The date is uncertain. Johnson, p. 350, says June 1861. Since it is one of the very few dates he bothers to give on this war, I suspect he must have some good authority for it. The earliest report on record is Hinderer to Venn, 2 Aug. 1861 (C.M.S. CA2/049).

some time his death was kept a close secret and even the missionaries did not report it. Abogunrin, his head slave who had become his chief official, and in recent months his spokesman, continued to act in collaboration with the Egba as if nothing had happened. During the whole of June, recruitment of soldiers was kept up at Abeokuta and fighting continued any time there was a break in the rains.[1] There was, for example, a great battle as late as 23 July.[2] But by the end of that month the rumour of the Are's death must have become widespread. At least it had reached the missionary at Ibadan. The chiefs at the Ibadan camp must also by then have become convinced that it was true. Balogun Ibikunle then took the first opportunity to open negotiations with the Egba to end the war since its major cause had now been removed. He was slow to realize that the character of the war had so changed that the removal of the Are made no difference to its continuation.[3] The only condition the Egba would accept was to be left in control of Ijaye, and this Ibadan found unacceptable.

There was a lull in the fighting as negotiation dragged on all that rainy season. The British change of front and the sudden annexation of Lagos constituted a menace to states with coastal interests, such as the Egba and Ijebu. These events, rather than driving the allies to make peace, only stiffened their determination to resist Ibadan to the last. Ibikunle who had never been convinced of the necessity of the war in the first place was loath to believe that it could still go on in spite of the Are's providential death. He therefore continued to negotiate patiently and meanwhile to put a brake on the fighting. The result of this policy was that by December the rainy season blues were again rampant in the Ibadan camp as Ogunmola boasted that but for the Balogun he would have finished the war long ago. Even the missionary at Ibadan shared the blues, grumbling about the Balogun prolonging the

---

[1] Bickersteth to Osborn, 6 June 1861 (M.M.S.), mentions notice from the Alake that all men who could carry a gun must go to war.

[2] Hinderer to Venn, 2 Aug. 1861 (C.M.S. CA2/049).

[3] *Ibid.* 27 Dec. 1861.

war unnecessarily: 'He has no doubt his reasons too for acting the part he does, but meanwhile he punishes everybody, friend and foe alike.'[1] By the end of January, the Balogun was obliged to break up negotiations and prepare to fight the war to a finish.

[1] Hinderer to Venn, 27 Dec. 1861 (C.M.S. CA2/049).

VI

THE FALL OF IJAYE

The Ibadan now decided on a close blockade of Ijaye. Early in February they moved their base from Olorisaoko, crossed the Ose and in the teeth of very strong resistance from the allies settled down within sight of the Ijaye walls. Balogun Ibikunle remained in charge of the camp. Ogunmola led a detachment of troops to a subsidiary camp farther west, overlooking the Egba camp and cutting off the line of communication between Ijaye and Abeokuta.[1] Ijaye troops were forced to come out and camp outside the walls, keeping an eye day and night on the Ibadan camp. Some sharp fighting followed these moves and it was becoming evident that Ibadan was getting the better of the fight. Not only were provisions getting short at the allied camps, but ammunition was also becoming exhausted. During February and March 1862 the missionary in Ibadan reported that every able-bodied man was being pressed to the war,[2] while the Egba could send no further reinforcements to the field.

This was not just because of the Ibadan blockade but even more because a huge Dahomey army was reported to be once again on the move for an invasion of Abeokuta. Throughout the month of March the Egba concentrated their energies at home, expecting the invasion. Early in March the invading army was reported in the Egba farms. Then the scouts brought the news that they had attacked Ishaga, an Egba town 15 miles west of Abeokuta. They had burnt it, captured all they could and were approaching the capital. Further news came to say they were returning westwards.[3] It was not till the end

[1] Johnson, p. 351; Mann, Journal, 10 Feb. 1862, in his account of the Last Days of Ijaye, dated London, 15 May 1862 (C.M.S. CA2/066).

[2] Hinderer to Venn, 1 March 1862 (C.M.S. CA2/049).

[3] Biobaku, p. 70; Champness to Hole, March 1865 (M.M.S.).

of the month that the Egba could be sure that the reported retreat was real and not feigned, and they were still waiting when
refugees started to arrive from Ijaye.

The Rev. Adolphus Mann, Anglican missionary at Ijaye,
began by the middle of February to fear not so much for his
own safety as for that of his wife who was expecting a baby.
She had chosen to remain with her husband when the other
missionary wives were evacuated. Mann had now come to the
conclusion that the end of Ijaye was near and that the chiefs
had better sue for peace. He therefore wrote a letter to the new
British Governor at Lagos, showing in what desperate circumstances Ijaye was, and asking him to intervene, indicating
that Ijaye chiefs were now so pressed that they would accept
terms.[1] He also wrote to his colleagues in Lagos to follow up
his letter to the Governor and to send someone to accompany
his wife down to the coast as he did not want to leave his flock
alone in their hour of need. He tried to get the chiefs to sign
a letter to the Governor, but they refused in spite of their difficulties, saying they would wait till after the first rains.[2] To sue
for peace then was to accept defeat. But if the allies could last
out the dry season, Ibadan would offer better terms to save
themselves spending another rainy season in the camp. But
the missionary put their refusal down as 'another instance of
that political arrogance their former master had instilled into
them'.

On Saturday, 15 March, the Governor's envoy, Lieutenant
Dolbein, arrived in Ijaye with a young Anglican catechist,
Edward Roper. The night before, hearing that they were on
the way, Mann had again summoned the chiefs to urge them to
surrender and get the British officer to negotiate peace terms,
but they did not turn up. They sent only one person to say that
they were not prepared to surrender in the way Mann was
suggesting. They however met Dolbein on his arrival and

[1] Mann, Last Days of Ijaye, dated London, 15 May 1862 (C.M.S. CA2/066);
Journal, 17 Feb., said he wrote the letter five weeks before. I think the date
should have been 17 March, so that he wrote the letter soon after the Ibadan
were encamped outside Ijaye, early in February.
[2] Ibid.

stated the justice of their cause in the war and again refused to sue for peace.[1] On the Sunday there was a fierce battle in which the allies were worsted, the Egba, it was said, having retreated prematurely. Dolbein prepared to leave for Lagos on Monday morning with Mrs. Mann. Edward Roper gallantly volunteered to stay behind in Ijaye so that Mann could accompany his wife.

The allied defeat that day and the demoralizing effect of the intended evacuation of the Manns, the last remaining Europeans, worried the allied chiefs. Would the people not panic and take their departure as an evil omen and the beginning of the end? They met that night in anxious council and decided to accept Dolbein's offer of mediation on Monday morning. When they arrived, Dolbein and the Manns were already packed to leave. They refused to delay their departure so as to embark on negotiation with Ibadan. They merely promised to pass on the chiefs' request to the Acting Governor in Lagos to use his influence to mediate as soon as possible. To allay the fears of the chiefs about the possible effects of their departure, Mann said that he was only taking his wife down to Lagos, that he would soon return and that in any case he was leaving someone else in his place. They left Ijaye by 11.00 a.m. First, a good number of women and children at Ijaye decided to join their caravan to Abeokuta. Then more and more began to feel it might be their last chance to escape from a doomed city. As the chiefs had foreseen, the departure of the Europeans was variously interpreted in Ijaye and the allied camps. Rumour spread. Rumour led to panic. That night there was a mass exodus of men, women and children from Ijaye. The Egba struck their camp quietly and moved off. Abogunrin himself led out the Ijaye.[2] By Tuesday morning, 18 March, when the Ibadan realized what was happening, the town had been largely deserted. Ibadan troops moved in and set it in flames.[3] Among the prisoners of war was Edward Roper, caught by soldiers from the household of Ogunmola. For his ransom,

---

[1] Mann, Journal, 15 March.   [2] *Ibid.* 16 and 17 March.
[3] Johnson, pp. 352–3.

Ogunmola insisted on 200 bags of cowries, 200 guns, and 200 kegs of gunpowder, but later released him free of charge on the Alafin's intervention.[1]

The Ibadan must have realized as much as anyone else that the fall of Ijaye in those circumstances did not mean the end of the war. By the end of March the Egba were just about ready to find outlet for the forces they had saved up to fight against Dahomey. The main Ijaye army, though badly shaken, had been evacuated from Ijaye, not annihilated there. The Ibadan therefore did not just break up camp and go home to celebrate victory. Probably anticipating that the allies might still have ambitions to hold the Upper Ogun, they sent the core of the Ibadan army under the younger generals to cross the Ogun and firmly establish Ibadan supremacy there. In particular, they laid siege to Awaye, which, with its natural fortifications, continued to defy the new conquerors. The Ibadan, no longer in the mood for an assault, laid siege to the town and decided to starve it out, a siege that was to last till October.[2]

The allies, however, did not intend to contest Ibadan supremacy in the Upper Ogun. The Ijaye war had been conclusive to the extent that in the rivalry for the control of the Oyo-speaking areas of the Yoruba country, Ijaye was now effectively eliminated. The ambitions of the Ijebu-Ode people and the Egba were to see that Ibadan did not become too powerful by increasing its power outside those areas. In particular, the Ijebu were anxious to reassert the control of the Awujale in Ijebu-Remo. The Egba were willing to help in this way to eliminate Ibadan's most important and most direct access to the coast. Both hoped to recoup some of their losses at Ijaye at the expense of the Remo people.

After the bulk of the Ijaye refugees had been settled in a new quarter on the eastern part of Abeokuta, the allies invaded Ijebu-Remo from both the Egba and the Ijebu sides some

---

[1] Johnson, p. 353; Hinderer to Lamb, Secretary C.M.S. Yoruba Mission, 24 March 1862 (C.M.S. CA2/049). Hinderer paid ransom for other mission agents, the Scripture Readers at Awaye and Ijaye and their families who were also captured.

[2] Johnson, p. 355; Hinderer to Lamb, 24 March 1862 (C.M.S. CA2/049).

time in May.[1] The two invading armies met outside Makun, one of the outposts on the route from Ikorodu to Ibadan. They laid siege to it in leisurely style, but within six weeks, probably on 19 June, the people opened their gates to avoid being starved out. Soon, prisoners of war were reported arriving in Abeokuta slave markets.[2] The allies occupied Makun and made it their principal base. They improved its fortifications and organized their supplies. Then the core of their armies moved to Iperu, a town friendly to the allies and whose rulers had invited them in. They similarly fortified Iperu and then moved towards Ipara, the most important town on the Ibadan route, the centre of the pro-Ibadan forces where the main resistance of Ijebu-Remo was now gathering.

Meanwhile, the Balogun of Ipara who had gone to Ibadan to rejoice with the victors hastened back to lead the resistance. The Ibadan were obliged to go to his aid, but they were at first divided as to whether to do this by going to Ipara and risk Ijebu-Igbo interfering with their supplies from Ibadan, or to attack Ijebu-Igbo first and risk the allies conquering Ijebu-Remo in the meantime. The rapid successes of the allies induced the Ibadan to choose the first alternative. Ogunmola led the remaining Ibadan troops from the Ijaye camp to Ipara. He personally supervised the collection of ammunition from Ikorodu through the enemy lines. Thus fortified, he marched out the troops against the allies hoping to capture their base at

[1] The Egba army probably moved out between 6 May (Champness to Osborn, talking only of peace. M.M.S.) and 9 May (Wood to Venn, first reporting the invasion. C.M.S. CA2/096). Wood adds that the missionaries 'were unanimous in condemning the movement, but could not stop it. Indeed, it was not known when the Abbeokutans went out where they were going.' Oral tradition in Ijebu-Remo attributes the conquest of Makun largely to the Egba, that the Awujale sent them to do it because it would have been contrary to convention for him to participate in an attack on a town he claimed to rule. This theory seems to have developed because the Remo people do not accept the punitive nature of the Awujale's expedition. The records and Okubote indicate that Ijebu-Ode took part.

[2] Champness to Osborn, 1 July 1862, and to Hole, 3 July 1862 (M.M.S.), reports the arrival of prisoners following the recent capture of 'Imakun', which agrees well with the date 19 July which Johnson, p. 356, gives for the destruction of Makun. The dates given by Okubote (7 April) and Losi, p. 72 (18 Aug.), are both clearly wrong. Ajisafe gives 19 June.

Iperu by storm. A hard-fought battle ensued. The Egba experience of resisting attacks, and the few cannon they had, were proof against Ogunmola's onslaught. The Ibadan had to withdraw with a notable loss of a number of important generals. They therefore decided to avoid more pitched battles in the meantime and to settle down to a siege.

With Ipara as their base, they fortified the main hills in the area, notably Oke Kere, as look-outs to guard their line of communication. The main bulk of the army encamped within two miles of Iperu on farms which they nick-named Aroma-mu, because of the great shortage of water. From Iperu the allied troops moved out from time to time to meet the Ibadan and try to drive them home. Kutuje, about a mile from the old Iperu walls, became the main theatre of the new phase of the war.[1] The Ibadan received reinforcements after the fall of Awaye in October, but fighting was kept down to a minimum as both sides waited for the dry season.

[1] Okubote; Akinyele, as well as oral tradition at Ipara and Iperu. In Ibadan, the Iperu phase of the war is known as Kutuje War.

VII

THE LAST PHASE

Inevitably, the campaign at Iperu was bound to be something of an anti-climax. As it settled down to a long siege featured by desultory fighting, it was soon obvious that most people were tired of the war. Neither Oyo nor Ijaye, the original principals of the Ijaye war, had any direct interest in the struggle for the control of Ijebu-Remo. It was essentially a domestic issue of the Ijebu people in which the Egba and the Ibadan had now become involved. The war had reached a stalemate. Neither side was willing or even able to continue the scale of exertions they had shown at Ijaye.

Ibadan was fighting under many disabilities in this new theatre of the war. The old Bale had died. The Balogun was incapacitated by illness. A number of other senior military and civil chieftaincies had been made vacant by deaths during the war.[1] The vacancies and the expectations of the changes to be involved in filling them considerably unsettled the politics of the town. The continuation of the war prolonged the malaise, especially since it kept in the camp Chief Ogunmola who had emerged as the strongest personality of the future. This was a serious handicap when the Ibadan were now fighting far from home and far from their farms, and with their lines of communication both with home and with the coast very much at the mercy of their enemies. The problem of maintaining a regular supply of provisions and ammunition was now a formidable exercise requiring strong political organization which the unsettled politics greatly weakened.

On the other hand, the allies were much more advantageously placed in this phase of the war. Like the Ibadan at Ijaye,

---

[1] Johnson, p. 357.

they were now fighting with their farms immediately to their rear and with their hold on the enemy's lines of communication. But the Egba in particular had other pre-occupations. They had their own constitutional crisis with the death of the Alake in September 1862 and the absence of an obvious choice for a successor. In the end, as a temporary compromise, the Basorun was named Regent, with much of the honour but without the title of king.[1] More serious was the relationship with the British which had been deteriorating since June 1861 and was approaching an inevitable crisis. The Egba were sore about the withdrawal of the promised military aid at the time they badly needed the aid. Even more deeply, they suspected the expanding power of the new British administration—the annexation of Badagry, Palma and Lekki, the protectorates over Ado and Okeodan—as a threat to their very independence.[2] The mission of Commander Beddingfield and Richard Burton to Abeokuta in November 1861 failed to satisfy them. The peremptory manner in which a Vice-Consul was posted to Abeokuta in July 1862 only heightened their fears.[3] On the British side, there was increasing frustration in the Lagos administration at the continuing war which interfered so much with trade and which no policy of theirs either of persuasion or of force could adequately deal with. Various attempts at mediation failed. The missionaries, reprimanded from London for their hitherto partisan role, attempted to unite with the educated traders in Lagos and mediate. In December 1862, the Rev. A. Lamb and Captain J. P. L. Davies, and in August 1862 the Rev. J. B. Wood and Mr Ashcroft, went up to Oyo hoping to start peace negotiations at the Ibadan end, but each time they failed.[4] In May 1863 the Acting Governor of Lagos, Captain Mulliner, and the naval Commodore Wilmot went up to Abeokuta, but they too failed to find the basis to

[1] Biobaku, p. 73.   [2] Newbury, pp. 69–70.
[3] Wood to Venn, 5 June 1862 (C.M.S. CA2/096); Champness to Osborn, 1 July 1862 (M.M.S.).
[4] Hinderer, Journal, Dec. 1862; Hinderer to Wood, 18 Aug. 1863; Hinderer to Venn, 29 Oct. 1863 (C.M.S. CA2/049); Wood to Venn, 4 Sept. 1863 (C.M.S. CA2/096).

negotiate a truce.[1] The suspicions on the Egba side and the frustrations on the British side complicated the difficulties inherent in the British annexation of Lagos and the imposition of a European administration on a state within a traditional African system of inter-state relationships, both political and economic. Acts of hostility followed on both sides. The Egba angrily expelled the Vice-Consul. The British encouraged Egba domestic slaves to flee to Lagos and take up service as porters or guards. The Egba retaliated by attacking transport caravans of British traders and officials, the British by proclaiming an arms blockade. The Egba closed the trade routes to Lagos, the British recalled all British subjects from Abeokuta, the Egba threatening to expel them any way. Thus the British, from a source of strength to the Egba, became a source of anxiety and a limiting factor on their activities at Iperu.

Besides this new pre-occupation of the Egba people, there was their old, permanent pre-occupation of the annual threat from Dahomey. In the dry season of 1863 there were reports that king Glele had definitely made up his mind for an invasion, that he had interpreted the earthquake that shook Accra on 10 July 1862 as the grumbling of his father in the invisible world and that he must be pacified with the blood of the Egba.[2] Thus again, all through March 1863, the Egba waited while their Christian friends in England, Canada, Syria and other places anxiously prayed for the survival of the town. The Dahomey were reported at Ibara on the opposite bank of the Ogun, but they withdrew without crossing.[3] They came, however, in March 1864 with an army of about 10,000. On the 15th they attacked the town, concentrating their forces on the Aro gate and trying to scale the walls in the face of heavy firing from the town. But they were repulsed. They made a stand

[1] Biobaku, p. 73; Champness to Osborn, 3 June 1863 (M.M.S.).

[2] Bickersteth to Osborn, 6 Sept. 1862 (M.M.S.).

[3] *C.M.I.* Vol. XIV, 1863. Champness to Osborn, 1 April 1863 (M.M.S.). The expected attack was widely publicized in missionary circles because, the peace mission of Commodore Wilmot to Dahomey having failed, the British Governor in Lagos advised missionaries at Abeokuta to flee from the town. The missionaries refused and prayed instead. They took the sudden withdrawal of Dahomey as a miraculous reply to their prayers.

just outside the Aro gate, the Egba having moved out to give battle. The Dahomey troops were forced to retreat with heavy losses. The Egba pursued them across the Ogun to beyond the ruins of Ishaga, and in the retreat the Dahomey suffered even heavier losses.[1] Once again the Egba had won, but the annual threat for long remained a dominant factor in Egba life every March as soon as the intervening rivers could be forded.

Elated by their victory of March 1864, the Egba moved extra troops to Makun. The Basorun himself went to the camp and attempted to finish the war by force.[2] The Ibadan were so hard pressed that Chief Ogunmola was reported to have summoned Balogun Ibikunle from his sick bed to come and lend the benefit of his experience in resisting the new allied offensive. The Ibadan were able to stand their ground.[3] And the war entered yet another rainy season, the fifth since the invasion of Ijaye. By then, both sides had seen just about enough of the war to be ready to make peace if it could be done without loss of face. In such circumstances, when the new revolutionary forces of army generals and strong-willed politicians had fought themselves to a stalemate, the traditional powers inherent in the monarchy, hitherto disregarded, came to the foreground.

Alafin Adelu, having for a long time lost control of the war he had such a large hand in starting, now began to pick up the reins again in negotiating a cease fire. When approached on earlier occasions by different peace missions from Lagos and other places, to use his influence to mediate in the war, he had merely referred the delegates to the Ibadan chiefs.[4] He was learning from experience to respect his father's view of the patient and dignified role of the monarch in a world of such turbulent towns and war chiefs, and to play the role with a

[1] Biobaku, p. 74.
[2] Sykes to Osborn, 9 June 1864 (M.M.S.), reported general conscription at Abeokuta. The war had been intensified.
[3] Johnson, p. 357.
[4] Hinderer to Wood, 18 Aug. 1863, and to Venn, 29 Oct. 1863 (C.M.S. CA2/049); Wood to Venn, 4 and 5 Sept. 1863, quoted Reid as saying that the Alafin was in favour of peace and that it was the Ibadan chiefs ('who used him more like a tool') who had turned down peace negotiations.

diplomatic finesse not unworthy of Atiba's son and successor. He had been in consultation all the time with other Yoruba monarchs, notably the Oni of Ife and the Alaketu of Ketu, both neutral but concerned about the possible outcome of the war. He had also kept in touch with developments at the battle front and in the main capitals. He realized the frustration at the continuation of the war and the growth of the peace party at Ibadan who had supported Balogun Ibikunle in opposing the war. He knew also that a new peace party was developing in Abeokuta, consisting largely of traders, crystallizing round Madam Tinubu, and now demanding a cessation of war and the opening of the trade routes.[1] Working through these two groups, the Alafin approached the war chiefs at the two camps to agree to a truce. It was agreed that he should send two deputations, one to the Ibadan camp, the other to the Egba camp with the emblems of Sango, to demand a three weeks' truce to allow the war chiefs on both sides to meet and negotiate terms and agree on a date to break up the camps. He did this and early in August the truce was proclaimed. Delegates from both sides met, apparently not to settle the issues in dispute—notably the allegiance of Ijebu-Remo people and the control of traffic through their country—but to settle the terms of an armistice to make it possible for both sides to withdraw without incidents and without one side using the opportunity to take advantage of the other. The peace settlement was to come later. The agreement was that on 25 August both sides were to break up their camps at Iperu, and on that day the Ibadan were to withdraw to Ipara and the Egba to Makun, both sides to disband and go home as soon after that as possible. Both sides swore to Sango to observe the terms. But as it turned out, the terms favoured the Egba much more than the Ibadan.[2] It was much easier for the allies to take advantage

<hr />

[1] Hinderer to Venn, 15 Nov. 1864 (C.M.S. CA2/049). For some impressions of Madam Tinubu see Broghero, Journal, 14 May 1864 (*Journal de la Mission du Dahomé* (SMA)). Fr Broghero visited Abeokuta from Whydah, 9–19 May 1864. He had travelled up under safe conduct provided for an Italian firm taking ammunition to the Basorun.

[2] Hinderer to Venn, 15 Nov. 1864; Johnson, pp. 358–60.

of the Ibadan at the time of withdrawal, the distance between Iperu and Makun being shorter than that between Iperu and Ipara.

The camps were broken up as arranged on 25 August but not without incidents. Egba troops who went to the camp at Aromamu were accused of falling on the Ibadan unawares and kidnapping a good number of them.[1] This delayed the conclusion of peace and made future negotiations of cease fires more complex. Nevertheless, the war had at last been brought to a stop, even if rather jerkily. The Ibadan and the Ijebu went home to settle their internal affairs. The Egba too went home, but not only to their internal problems. Their crisis with the British continued to grow and soon involved them in yet one more battle that may be regarded as the tail piece of the Ijaye war.

Throughout the battle at Iperu, the Ikorodu people continually smuggled arms to Ipara and on occasions raided the allied camp at Makun.[2] Now they were saying openly that they had no intention of returning to their allegiance to the Awujale. This issue could, by itself, have been dealt with as part of the general peace settlement, the allies trying to get the connivance of Ibadan, if necessary, to coerce Ikorodu on condition that the route be kept open subject to tolls being paid to the Awujale.[3] But the issue became involved in the Egba dispute with the British administration in Lagos. Lagos had a vital interest in keeping open the Ikorodu market as a mart for interior traders. And because of the naval force at his disposal, the Lagos Governor had often declared that the market was under the special protection of Lagos. When Captain John Glover, the dynamic and ambitious Governor of Lagos, visited the Egba camp at Makun in June 1864, just before the armistice, he had promised to allow the allies to coerce Ikorodu provided they could do it quickly and without interfering

---

[1] Hinderer to Venn, 15 Nov. 1864; Johnson, pp. 358–60; also Sykes to Hole, 4 Oct. and 5 Nov. 1864 (M.M.S.).

[2] Ajisafe, p. 72.

[3] This was the term of peace suggested by Glover when he visited the Makun camp (Glover to Russell, 6 Sept. 1864. P.R.O. FO84/1221).

with trade.[1] After the armistice, the Egba even more than the Ijebu were anxious to carry out the coercion largely to curb the expansionist attitude of the Lagos Governor who was beginning to claim that the British owned not just Lagos island as the original proclamation had expressed, but also an undefined strip of the mainland described as Lagos 'farms'.[2] The Egba saw in the British control of the Ikorodu market a dangerous enclave on the mainland that could easily spread up the Ogun river towards them. They moved out quietly to Ikorodu in November and laid siege, forgetting that with naval power the British could do in Ikorodu what they wished but could not do at Makun or Ijaye. Glover soon began to demand, at first quite gently, then in increasingly peremptory a manner, that the Egba should withdraw. In March he issued an ultimatum to the Egba to withdraw within 24 hours or be dislodged. The Egba paid no heed to the ultimatum. On 29 March a carefully prepared expedition with a core of about 250 troops from the Fourth and Fifth West India Regiments and the Hausa Constabulary, armed with such weapons as bayonets, shells and rockets, and supported by Ikorodu and Ibadan friends, attacked the Egba besiegers. Their camp was set ablaze, and as they retreated in confusion, pursued by the Ikorodu and Ibadan auxiliaries, the shells and rockets took heavy toll of Egba lives. Thus the Egba were driven home.[3]

The Ibadan justified their joining Glover at Ikorodu on the grounds that the Egba had themselves broken the terms of the armistice by the incidents at the Aromamu camp the previous August. Wrangling had been going on for some time over those incidents, and the Ibadan had refused to discuss peace until they had taken their revenge. Early in March they sacked Atade, an Egba caravanserai, some eight miles from Abeokuta, and then went from there to join the British in raising the siege of Ikorodu. Thus satisfied, they were willing to discuss peace. Eventually, peace was made in July 1865, with an exchange of

[1] Glover to Russell, 6 Sept. 1864 (P.R.O. FO84/1221).
[2] Biobaku, pp. 75–6. Glover apparently succeeded in detaching the Awujale from joining the Egba at Ikorodu.
[3] Biobaku, p. 76.

notable prisoners and mutual opportunities for ransoming relations captured in the war. The roads between the major towns were formally declared open. Perhaps the question of the Ibadan route to the coast was also settled, but it was soon obvious that a satisfactory solution had not yet been arrived at.

The missionaries announced that, as part of the formal opening of roads, the routes to the coast were also open. However, they were obliged to modify this statement in April 1866, to the effect that there were serious qualifications in Ibadan's freedom of access to the sea. The Ibadan were not disputing the Awujale's suzerainty over Ijebu-Remo. What they wanted was ready access to the coast even if subject to the payment of tolls. The allies, it would appear, were ready to allow access only in special cases. Rather, they wanted to build up Berekodo on the Egba side and Iperu on the Remo side as markets where Ibadan would normally export their produce and receive goods from the coast. This of course would have put a severe limitation on Ibadan's access to ammunition.

The matter of Ibadan's access to the coast could no longer be viewed by the Egba and Ijebu in terms of Ibadan's power alone, but now also in terms of Ibadan's alliance with Lagos and the increasing threat of British expansion from Lagos. As long as the Egba and Ijebu were able, they determined to use their position on the coast to defend their sovereignty and to keep out British infiltration. The Ijebu, who had not in the past encouraged much intercourse with Europeans, withdrew into a rigid isolation with a complete ban on Europeans. The Egba who had welcomed many European missionaries and traders began to move in a similar direction. On Sunday, 13 October 1867, a spontaneous riot developed into a mass attack on all European missionaries and traders alike, as a result of which they were expelled from Abeokuta. It was not till 1875 that this ban on Europeans at Abeokuta was relaxed. In the case of Ijebu, the British in 1892 had to force their way in. Meanwhile, Glover recognized the completeness of the ban and from 1872 onwards tried to open a new route from Lagos down the lagoon to Agbabu, and from there, inland to

Ondo, and then either westwards through Okeigbo and Ife to Ibadan or northwards through Ekiti to Ilorin and the Niger.

Similarly the Ijaye war had failed to solve the crisis in the interior of the Yoruba country. Ijaye town had been eliminated and Ibadan emerged stronger than before. But Kutuje had shown that Ibadan could be fought to a standstill. The later success of the Egba–Ijebu alliance thus considerably redressed the balance of power which the fall of Ijaye had upset, especially since they were also successful in containing British penetration for the meantime. The Egba had also defeated Dahomey and were now in a position even to interfere in Porto Novo politics. Perhaps the most significant result of the elimination of Ijaye was that the basis of the Oyo–Ibadan alliance was considerably weakened. Oyo inherited most of the Upper Ogun districts taken from Ijaye, excepting the Ibarapa district which Ibadan took. Oyo thus emerged from the war greatly strengthened and increasingly impatient with the overbearing manners of its supposed vassal, Ibadan. In theory, Ibadan continued to acknowledge the suzerainty of the Alafin. In practice, rather than be dictated to from Oyo, Ibadan sought to exert considerable influence on what happened at Oyo, while it continued to extend its powers in the Ijesha, Ekiti, and Akoko districts. When eventually in 1877 Ogedengbe led the Ekiti resistance against Ibadan, he had the overt support of Ilorin, Ife, Ijebu and Egba, and the not so overt support of the Alafin. The Kiriji War which ensued was thus a new phase in the struggle for supremacy in the Yoruba country. Like the Ijaye War, Kiriji was to end in stalemate. By then, however, the British were ready to interrupt the struggle by assuming the supremacy themselves.

VIII

CONCLUSION

One of the reasons why the efforts of the British officials in Lagos in trying to mediate in the Ijaye War were so ineffective was that they did not understand what the war was all about. Since they were themselves pre-occupied with the problem of protecting the commercial interests of Britain, they had a natural predilection for seeing West Africa in economic terms. They argued that the basic issues in the Ijaye War, as in the Yoruba wars generally, were economic. The object of the Egba, said McCoskry in 1861, was 'in reality to obtain a monopoly of commerce by closing all the roads from Lagos into the interior except that by Abeokuta'.[1] A year later, talking of the Ikorodu–Ibadan route, Glover declared: 'This road, my lord, is the sole object of the war.'[2]

Underlying this view was the over-simplification of life in West Africa as portrayed by the anti-slavery propaganda of the first half of the nineteenth century. In the abolitionist view, African wars were the result, not of unresolved political problems, but of the slave trade and the consequent social and moral degeneration of the Africans. The wars, in fact, were not manly and heroic wars as known in Europe, but 'interminable slave raids'. As an English friend of Anna Hinderer said of the Ijaye War: 'War having once begun, it dragged on its slow and varying course in characteristic African style, through many successive years. It was, in fact, war without many battles, and was rather a state of hostility, treachery, lying in wait for stragglers and capturing prisoners for slaves.'[3] Since little was known of the politics, the slave trade was used

[1] McCoskry in his handing over notes to Governor Freeman, enclosed in Freeman to Russell, 4 June 1862 (P.R.O. FO84/1175).

[2] Glover to Russell, 9 June 1863 (P.R.O. FO84/1210).

[3] Comment by the editor in Anna Hinderer, p. 216.

as the principal explanation of both the origin and the long duration of the Yoruba Wars. To stop the wars, no political solution need be offered; only economic, social and moral improvement through 'legitimate' and 'free' trade, Christianity and civilization. And because historians have tended to accept this simplified economic interpretation too readily, the politics behind the wars have been neglected.[1]

It seems obvious that the role of trade generally and the slave trade in particular in the Yoruba Wars has been grossly exaggerated. There is no basis for the view that 'one of the principal reasons why the provincial chiefs broke away from Oyo control was that they wanted a larger share of the profits of the slave trade than the Alafin and his court officials were prepared to allow'.[2] Rather, the evidence points to the view that the slave trade in the Yoruba country was inconsiderable before 1820.[3] The great expansion of the trade in the 1820's, and the consequent growth of Lagos and Badagry as important centres of the slave trade were the result, not the cause, of the collapse of the Old Oyo empire. It is true that we do not know for certain what caused the rift between the Alafin and the Basorun, the other chiefs, generals and provincial rulers, but we can make a more convincing guess than that it was a quarrel over the profits of the slave trade. An empire of that size, with its loose organization, inadequate communication and lack of homogeneity, had within itself the seeds of conflict and disruption. The desire of the Dahomey or the Egba to stop paying tribute to Old Oyo can be explained by the natural desire for political autonomy.

Similarly, the wars that followed can be explained in terms of the political problems posed by the disappearance of the empire without relying so heavily on the slave trade theory. The fall of Old Oyo had left a power vacuum in the Yoruba

---

[1] Cf. Burns, p. 127: 'The dispute between the Ibadan and the Egbas was mainly economic.' Also Fage, p. 91: 'The social canker which had beset Yorubaland was only finally checked by the imposition of external authority and the introduction of new social doctrines in the form of British rule and Christian missions.'

[2] Fage, p. 90.   [3] Biobaku, pp. 12–13; Newbury, p. 36.

country and the basic cause of the wars was the desire of several of the successor states to fill the vacuum. As a missionary at Oyo put it in 1860: 'To re-establish the Yoruba kingdom and make it what it once was, I am quite certain, is the grand cause of this war.'[1] Since none of the states was succeeding well enough to achieve this, there was the more immediate desire of the different states, each to protect itself and make sure that the balance of power among the states was not redressed to its own particular disadvantage. Each successive war may be regarded as a desire to re-examine that balance and to re-establish it. The Ijaye War in particular was an attempt on the part of Oyo and Ibadan to weaken Ijaye and the consequent resistance of Ijaye, Abeokuta and ultimately Ijebu-Ode to such an attempt on the grounds that it would leave Ibadan dangerously powerful.

Admittedly, economic considerations featured prominently in this struggle. The basic ingredients of power were land and taxable peasants. Each state sought to win control over as many towns and villages as possible, and to tax them. It also tried to capture slaves in war who were valuable both for work on the farms and service in the ranks of the armies. Thus the Ijaye War was a struggle for the control of the Upper Ogun and Ijebu-Remo in which the desire for economic exploitation was an important element. But to see in the war merely an economic struggle 'to obtain a monopoly of commerce' is to miss the essential political motivation, and to exaggerate the importance of trade in nineteenth-century Yoruba states. The basis of the life of the states was agriculture, and commerce as an ingredient of power ranked much lower in them than the British officials estimated.

The question then arises as to why the trade routes played such a prominent part in the Ijaye War. And this links up with the particular problem of the role of the slave trade as a medium of exchange for ammunition. It is still a very controversial question. T. J. Bowen, the American missionary, a keen observer of Yoruba war and politics said: 'once begun

[1] Reid to Taylor, 17 June 1860 (S.B.C.).

for political reasons [the wars] have commonly been nourished by the slave trade'.[1] Professor Fage puts it more strongly: 'the existence of the ready market provided by the European traders for the sale of slaves and the purchase of guns made it virtually impossible for the Yorubas to return to a more peaceable way of life unaided'.[2]

It should be noticed that in the different Yoruba states, the buying of ammunition was state-controlled, and so was the slave trade involved in the transactions. Thus, if the slave trade 'nourished' the wars, in the sense of providing ammunition, then the slave trade was still subordinate to the political issues that gave rise to the necessity for providing ammunition. The slave trade was important only as long as slaves were the most marketable commodity. Indeed, it is doubtful whether, by the time of the Ijaye war, slaves continued to be very important for the purchase of arms. From the fragmentary evidence at our disposal, it would appear that Ikorodu and Lagos were the most important markets for buying the ammunition used in this war. According to Newbury, between July 1862 and the end of 1864, £23,000 worth of arms and powder was imported into Lagos.[3] The size of this importation would seem to have been a response to the demands of the war. But both Lagos and Ikorodu were under the surveillance and control of the British and there has been no suggestion that slave trade was going on to any great extent on the Lagos lagoon or in Lagos itself at this time. Ammunition was being bought for cash or in exchange for agricultural produce. Thus 'legitimate' trade was rising but this did not itself end the wars because the political issues remained independent of the slave trade, and they remained unsolved.

There was, however, the selling of slaves, not for the acquisition of ammunition from European sources, but for profit. This continued much longer, because when the external market became restricted, slaves began to be directed more and more to the internal market. The growth of 'legitimate' commerce was itself an important factor in extending

[1] Bowen, p. 113.   [2] Fage, p. 91.   [3] Newbury, pp. 72–3.

the internal market for the labour of domestic slaves. This internal slave trade was not controlled and it operated largely on commercial lines. It sometimes produced indiscriminate slave-raiding during wars begun for political ends, because the chiefs, collectively or individually, desired to make profit from wars. This was the case of the Egba at Ijaye and Makun and Kutuje, but it was largely because their basic objective, the recovery of their land, had eluded them. Even then, this profit motive was still subordinated to the other objective of clipping the wings of Ibadan. Very rarely did the profit motive take precedence over the political issues.

Thus, if the trade routes featured prominently in the Ijaye war, it was not because of the desire to capture commerce. Indeed, the Egba usually showed a willingness to subordinate trade to their political objectives by legislating for the suspension of trade in order to compel young men to go to war. Rather, it was because in any serious war the control of the lines of communication is a crucial factor and trade routes were required in times of war to protect not just the supply of ammunition, but also the provision of food. The former is often enough stressed, but hardly ever the latter. As it turned out in the Ijaye war, interference with the food supply could be more effective against an opponent than the interference with the supply of ammunition.

Finally, we can only briefly allude here to the social and political consequences of the Ijaye war within each of these states. Many writers on the Yoruba wars imagine a 'general holocaust', when 'the harassed peasant had little time for agriculture or trade'.[1] This picture is not supported by the evidence on the Ijaye war, possibly the most bitterly fought Yoruba war of the nineteenth century. There were serious war privations. In the case of Ijaye, there was much suffering from famine. And then the town was completely destroyed, the population having to start life all over again, either as slaves or as free men in other towns and villages. But life went on. Agriculture was maintained over wide areas. In spite of

[1] Burns, p. 28.

the closure of roads and formal laws prohibiting trade, much commercial traffic went on, largely through smuggling by people supposed to be buying and selling ammunition. There were always state-escorted caravans connecting the main centres. In 1861, Hinderer went to Lagos with an Ibadan caravan which went to buy arms.[1] In 1864, Broghero went to Abeokuta with three large canoes loaded by an Italian firm in Lagos, escorted up the river Ogun by officials of the Basorun. The canoes contained largely ammunition, but there were several other trade goods passed off as the provisions of the missionary.[2]

And just as there was no general holocaust, life did not remain static. The idea of a classical form of Yoruba institutions and political systems, divorced from the politics of the nineteenth century and unchanged till the advent of British rule, is false. War on the scale we have been describing, the fall of a town of the size and importance of Ijaye, the evacuation of people from one place to another, the rise and fall of ambitious and dominant personalities, all these and other factors produced changes to which the different States constantly tried to adjust their politics and administrative machines.

[1] Hinderer to Venn, 10 March, 23 April 1861 (C.M.S. CA2/085).

[2] Broghero, *Journal de la Mission du Dahomé,* entries for 1 to 21 May 1864 (S.M.A.). Broghero mentions a visit to Madam Tinubu, her wealth and influence and how she was preparing to go to the war camp at Makun. It is likely that, following the ruin of her trade in Lagos and her expulsion, it was largely during the Ijaye War that she built up her wealth.

APPENDIX

CAPTAIN JONES'S REPORT ON THE EGBA ARMY IN 1861

Captain Arthur Trefusis Jones was an officer of the Second West India Regiment stationed in Sierra Leone. Consul Foote of Lagos sent Jones to report on the capabilities of the Egba army. He reached Abeokuta in May 1861 and later visited the Egba war camps at Olokemeji and Ijaye. The report was written on his return to Abeokuta at the end of May.

Meanwhile, Consul Foote had died and his acting successor, McCoskry, asked Jones to undertake a mission to Ibadan and Oyo to investigate the chances of negotiating a peace.

Jones had already suffered one attack of fever and during this second journey the illness recurred. Jones died on 7 July 1861, without completing his mission.

Report addressed to the Officer Commanding the Second West Indian Regiment, Sierra Leone[1]

Abbeokuta
June 6th 1861

Sir,

In compliance with the orders of Commodore Edmonstone, dated Lagos April 29th a duplicate of which I have enclosed, directing me to proceed to this place 'with the view of obtaining all the military information as to the resources of the Country, and the means' the Abbeokutans 'may have of carrying on an offensive war, for the better guidance of Her Majesty's Government,' I have the honour to report that I started from Lagos on the 7th May, I was prevented making an earlier start from illness consequent on exposure in the River and Lagoon during the expedition to Porto Nuovo. I reached this City on Saturday May 11th and received audience of the Alake or King, on the morning of the 13th.

Nothing could be more gracious than my reception, and every facility was promised to enable me to carry out the objects for which I had been despatched hither, and on my expressing my desire to have an opportunity of making a full and complete inspection of

[1] Enclosed in Consular Despatch no. 17 of 20 June 1861 from Governor Hill at Sierra Leone to Lord John Russell (P.R.O. FO84/1134).

the Troops composing His Majesty's Army, I was informed that it was at present engaged actively in the field, but that in the event of my deciding upon visiting their camps, I should be furnished with letters to the Chiefs and generals, who would be instructed to give me every assistance for acquiring the information desired. Furnished with these credentials, I started on 17 May for the camp of observation at Okemeji, distant about 30 miles. Ogobono the General who defeated the Dahomian army in 1851, is in command here, the position being one of great importance, being so placed as to cut off communication between the enemy and the coast. Here I remained three days taking every opportunity of making myself acquainted with the various subjects incidental to native Camps, their construction, maintenance etc. From thence I proceeded to Ijaye, about 40 miles in a northerly direction, where are the camps of the Egbas and Ijayes. The Abbeokutans are an integral portion of the Egba tribe, these two tribes have united against the Ibadans. I started for camp early on the morning of 22nd May and rode the entire distance, passing through the enemies' country, who having heard of my intended visit by means of spies, had sworn to sacrifice me. However by taking this journey and riding on ahead of the Escort provided for me, I was enabled to forestall their intentions, and reached the camp late the same evening.

As the results prove, it is fortunate in other respects that I acted thus, in what might otherwise appear a rash and unnecessary manner for on the day after my arrival a battle took place, from which it was hoped by the Ibadans some good would result before the 'fetish' or charm of the white man's presence could operate against them. During the engagement I took up a position nearly amongst the front rank, and about 300 yards distance from the enemy. I was thus enabled to watch the tactics of both sides with great facility. I was however reluctantly compelled to withdraw, my Interpreter being wounded by my side in the thigh, my own leg grazed by a bullet, and a 3rd bullet striking the tree against which we were leaning, a few inches above my head.

However I had seen sufficiently by that time to enable me subsequently to follow all their movement from a spot a little further retired.

I remained at this point until the action was over; it terminated in a drawn battle with little loss on either side. My visit to their Camp extended to the morning of 29th May, when I retraced my steps, arriving at Abbeokuta on the 31st ultimo.

I have thus placed before you a Summary of my proceedings since my departure from Lagos at which place the Detachment 2nd W.I. Rgt. still remains, according to the instructions contained in the letter before mentioned.

However with regard to these men I may state that on my first arrival I endeavoured to ascertain whether they could be employed in the manner proposed originally, but I received no direct reply to my queries on the subject. I was directed to put myself in communication with the General in Camp. Notwithstanding I have repeatedly urged the matter and pointed out the positive advantages to be gained by acquiescing in my suggestions I have failed to obtain any more satisfactory results than 'promises' to provide recruits and accommodation for the men.

As promises here are like their acts remarkable for the frequency of their repetition but slowness of performance I have not thought myself warranted in bringing up the Detachment until I see more zeal and appreciation of the offer manifested by the Authorities.

If the same lukewarm state of affairs obtains at the period of sailing of the next mail, it is my intention to forward them to Sierra Leone.

Although forming no part of my duty, to take cognizance of such matters, I conceive it right that the Government should be put in possession of the fact, that the presents of guns and ammunition made at various times to the Alake intended for the defence of Abbeokuta are now lying in different parts of the City without the slightest regard being had for their preservation exposed to all the inclemency of the rainy season, whereby the carriages are part decaying, and the various accessories are either lost or broken, or afford daily amusement to the ragged or naked urchins who roam about at will.

The gun lately presented to them, and which accompanied me up the river, is being treated in the same way, opportunity is thus afforded me to address the Alake on the subject, and I shall not fail to express to him what I conceive will be the feeling of Her Majesty's Government viz the sorrow and indignation at the scorn and indifference thus manifested towards their endeavours to make them secure against attacks from their enemies.

Appended to this, in the form of a Report, are the observations I have made and the facts I have collected on the subject of the Abbeokutan Military Forces, a form I have adopted more for convenience of reference.

Trusting that the manner in which I have so far performed the responsible duties entrusted to me will meet with the approbation of Her Majesty's Government and be to your satisfaction.[1]

Report on the Constitution and Military Capability of the Abbeokutan Army for carrying on an offensive war.[2]

Before proceeding to a description of the Military Forces of this Power, it will be necessary to give a brief description of the Constitution.

Abbeokuta is the name applied to a collection of Towns each of them the nucleus, or rather residue of a tribe which depopulated and expelled in former times by internecine or general war from its ancient farms and hereditaments was compelled to fly and ultimately settling down in a rocky district founded a new town and colony called after the former one.

Each of these tribes retained in its integrity, its institutions, customs and superstitions.

Over them all collectively at the present date expanded to a very considerable extent presides an hereditary ruler, called the Alake unable to exercise independent authority yet capable of expressing a veto upon propositions from the chiefs, who rule their respective tribes but his assent is necessary to legalise all acts affecting the general welfare. In all questions therefore in order to obtain the voice of the people the chief who is elected to that position by popular voice from his warlike capacity and may therefore be considered the head warrior of his tribe, assembles the 'Obonis' or Elders and states the case, gives his views, his opinion or wish to them; they then retire and having deliberated return to give him the decision at which they have arrived.

The result the chief ultimately states in an assembly of chiefs, and if these should not obtain unanimity, the majority carry the day, and their decision being carried to the Alake whose object is naturally to comply with the wish of the majority, he usually assents to their proposals.

Under such a form of Government there does not exist a standing army. The question of war is generally decided in public at what is called an 'Oio' or an extraordinary meeting held in the open air for the purpose of obtaining an expression of public opinion and passing certain edicts in conformity with that opinion. When the

[1] This was signed by A. A. Harrison, M.B., on 7 June, as Captain Jones was ill with fever and had no time to finish his correspondence for the mail.

[2] Enclosed in War Office letter of 29 Aug. 1861 to Foreign Office (P.R.O. FO84/1155).

'Oio' takes place, women are confined to their houses, no matter what is its duration, the limit however is three days. At these meetings the Chiefs, Obonis and members of the Tribes all collect in a circle, sometimes to the number of thousands and everyone is allowed the expression of his opinion thro' the Elders or Chief of his Tribe.

The Speaker stands in the centre and delivers his opinion. I was present at an Oio held in Abbeokuta a short time ago to decide a question connected with the present war, and was much struck with the regularity of the proceedings and the decorum which prevailed. Having thus briefly sketched an outline of the constitution of this kingdom:—

Let us now suppose that war is declared, the question naturally arises, How is an army raised? Orders are issued to each chief to collect his warriors, also to pay into the Public Treasury a contribution towards the Expenses of the war, and to repair with his men on a fixed day to a rendezvous. It resolves itself into a question of Clanship, for although each Chief permanently possesses a few men called warriors, they are his body guard in times of peace, are employed solely on State occasions, and carrying messages of importance to the different chiefs, they are confidential men, a sort of Privy Council, and the Servants partake of their meals occasionally with him.

With the exception of these few armed retainers the remainder of the Tribe are almost without exception Farmers or engaged in peaceful occupations. They are docile, obedient to command, capable of enduring great bodily fatigue and marching with ease 40 miles a day with loads on their heads, the usual method for carrying burdens in this country, but once armed and their passions roused, like all nations low in the intellectual scale, they become fierce and blood-thirsty, mangling their unfortunate victims in a fight like the veriest savages. By a system of voluntary enlistment the Abbeokutan army is raised, but often extreme measures are resorted to as in the case of the present war, where, at the 'Oio' before mentioned an edict was passed that whosoever did not proceed at once to the war should be deprived of his heart.

Arrived at the rendezvous the chiefs are placed under the orders of a general, himself always the head of a Tribe, and according to his directions they take the Field. Of the numerical strength of his forces he is however altogether ignorant, as I know from personal observation and frequent enquiry. As many of the head chiefs are extremely powerful and wealthy, the number, though never accurately known, that they bring into the field are considerable and having chiefs under them the total may be looked upon as a Brigade and the subordinate chiefs as commanding regiments, and much in this way they are used on active service.

The fighting men are supposed to arm themselves which they do according to their means. The army now in the field with the exception of an almost infinitesimal proportion are all armed with guns, which are ordinarily called the 'Long Dane' costing 21s. 6d., but the State finds them with a proportion of powder, which is very coarse.

The bullets are made out of bar iron, of variable diameter some being merely bolts, other ranging from the size of grape down to brick shot. Each chief has now got a few pieces fired from rests with a bore of about $1\frac{1}{2}$ inches into which they put a handful of bullets and with these at close quarters they sometimes do great execution, all these firearms are of the flint period and are of very rough manufacture.

But a very small proportion of the Abbeokutan army is armed with swords indeed the use of firearms appears to have thrown the hand to hand conflicts out of fashion, as a general mode of warfare, but such as use them do not appear to me to take a very active part in the conflict, but rather wait for an opportunity of cutting off their man, upon whom even after death they wreak their vengeance by hacking and hewing the dead body.

The swords are always straight, double-edged, about 3ft long.

I remember in action at Ijaye, that the swordsmen were generally armed with a pistol as a supplementary weapon. I saw but very few spearmen and but an occasional bow and arrow.

In fighting they are not naked, but wear a sort of 'trews' and a war jacket of a striped, red, blue and white pattern invariably loose, cut away at the shoulders and low at the neck; over this they carry their ball bag and powder flask which is made out of a gourd which grows here in great profusion, this is suspended from the right shoulder and hangs at the left side.

Most of the warriors wear 'gree-gree' or charms—some of the principal men wear elaborately marked war dresses, studded with cowries and the teeth of wild animals. Cavalry does not exist as a separate branch of the military service, but some few mounted men are generally present in the field, they are however men of rank generally bringing 2 or 3 retainers with them.

The [horsemen] appear to be used by the generals chiefly in carrying orders and bringing up stragglers. As Horses are numerous and hardy, requiring little attention and feeding on grass a very excellent irregular cavalry might be speedily organized.

The Abbeokutans are in possession of 7 guns of various calibres, supplied to them from time to time by the English Government, and a large supply of ammunition, but the advance of civilization up to the present has not enabled these men to appreciate the value of artillery. So indifferent and careless are the governing powers and even the missionaries to whose care the guns have in some instances been confided by the Alake to the preservation of these articles that one of the guns a brass 6 lb. field piece has been lying out in the open air for many months in the yard of the Church Missionary Society, a roost for cocks and hens exposed to all the vicissitudes of climate until one of the wheels has rotted, and the gun could not consequently travel a mile over the roads of the country without breaking down, while many of its appurtenances are taken, permanently injured or lost. Still further as illustrating the blindness and want of appreciation of these gifts and their utility—I must mention that the small detachment of gunners of the 2nd W.I. Reg. which accompanied me, and were left at Lagos until I could procure suitable accommodation for them in Abbeokuta, and ascertain whether it was probable that the Government would hand over to me men for instruction in gunnery, still remains at that port in consequence of the supineness and insensibility of the Authorities to the advantages placed before them.

It might naturally be supposed that the State would make some provision for its protectors when in the field, but no such theory obtains here. Each fighting man from the Chief downwards feeds himself according to his own taste and fancies or means. To enable them to do this many of those who during time of peace have farms or other means of livelihood lay in supplies of corn which they retail to others: their wives whom they take with them to camp, sit in the market and sell for the public weal. Almost a certain measure or otherwise of the supplies lies in the fact that as the chiefs are men of most substance and possessing many wives, these who sit also in the market will naturally sell according as they find the store houses getting empty and place such a price on the staple articles of food such as cassada [sic] etc. as will indicate the supply.

Moreover if a man having served some time at the war finds his supplies getting low, he quietly shoulders his firelock and returns to his home, until by work or otherwise, he acquires money enough to purchase a fresh supply of provisions, or a new harvest has replenished his barns.

During my recent [visit?] to the camps of Okemeji and Ijaye I had daily opportunities of seeing the mode in which the inhabitants of these regions protect themselves against the vicissitudes of climate, the heat of the tropical sun, the dews of midnight, and the torrents of a tornado. Here may I observe that they go to war in a very systematic manner as regards their present comforts: it cannot be more appropriately described than by adducing the scriptural phrase of a nation 'going out to war, sitting down and encamping against a Town'. They seldom or ever form their camps in the open country one or other [sic], but generally both are in sight of the Town selected for attack. In the present instance of the war between the Ibadans and Egbas, the former came up against Ijaye: encamped close to it within ¾ hour's march, building regular villages, making farms and planting corn: in the same way the Egbas going to the assistance of the Ijayes encamped outside the walls of the town, laid out a regular Town, with farms etc. They seldom shift their ground for this reason, and their wars consequently are wars of procrastination, and manœuvering by means of lies, deceit and spies.

Their mode of encampment is as follows: in the neighbourhood of a suitable soil, mud huts generally obtain, of an oblong form and divided into 3 equal parts, the centre for a reception apartment and open to the front: the two ends being used, the one for sleeping and the other for a store. The vast majority of the huts are on this principle, but at times the rank of the individual entitles him to enlarge and even enclose his dwelling within a sort of court yard. Where clay does not exist, recourse is had to the forest for materials, and of these there is no lack, for except near the Towns 'bush' abounds in the greatest profusion. Their mode of construction is simple in the extreme, but serviceable beyond belief, in fact they appear capable of withstanding the inclemency of the season, with but occasional repairs, for 2 or 3 years.

They proceed as follows: 1st by cutting two stout poles about 6 ft high and forked; they form the extremity of the building by placing the forked end uppermost, next 4 stout poles are selected, also forked. These make the four corners, while according to the fancy of the builder, any number of light ordinary poles may be placed at intervals between them to form the supports.

The next step consists in laying in the forked extremities of the uprights, 3 poles lengthways the same length as the building intended, one from each corner and the 3rd along the centre, about 18ft in length, the rafters follow next in succession, and are formed of young bamboes [sic], the roof itself being procured from 2 large species of grass or bamboe leaves with which the building being thatched and walled in, the whole is rendered perfectly watertight.

So much for the individual houses; there does not appear to be any regularity in the laying out of the camp, no regular streets or divisions.

As might be expected, the men from the same tribe live as near to [one] another as possible in the same quarter, so as to be under the control of their chief.

For the protection of the camp as well as for its supply the site is chosen if possible near or on the bank of a stream—further, and this appears to be the extent of their engineering powers, it is surrounded by a deep ditch and parapet, the former is often extremely formidable, being much deeper in proportion than is usually admitted in systematic engineering, considering the height of the latter, the faults are however numerous, as might be expected where scientific principles are not called into play, the principal ones being, that sufficient width is not given to the ditch, no slope is given to the scarp, the parapet is not sufficiently high, being seldom more than 4 or 5ft high, without a banquette, its thickness is not sufficient being generally not more than 12–18 inches, and its stability is further weakened . . . . . . which are too frequent and invariably round.

The top of the parapet is thatched with the same materials as their huts, and being sloped, the rain rolls off it, whereby much harm to the wall is prevented, which it would otherwise sustain, from the heavy rains prevalent at certain seasons.

As to a further means of guarding against surprises, in places where the camp does not happen to be situated on high ground 'watch Towers' are raised on scaffolding varying in height according to the nature of the ground to be overlooked, in which sits a sharp and intelligent sentinel whose duty it is to report the least movement of the enemy's troops, or unusual excitement in his camp.

I may mention here the fact that most of the Generals and chiefs are provided with either reconnoitering glasses or telescopes with the use of which they are quite familiar.

Having thus given an outline of the principal points in connection with the raising and equipment of the native army and also described their Commissiariat in the field, and mode of encampment, I proceed to describe as far as the opportunity afforded me by the battle of Ijaye May 23rd 1861 will admit their tactics, and mode of warfare.

The first move in a campaign appears to be to set abroad as many deceitful Reports as possible with regard to its objects and intentions and at the same time to endeavour to acquire by means of spies and bribery, all the information possible, as to the strength etc. of the enemy's forces; as a general rule the opposite party are aware of the intention to make an attack or offer battle and are therefore fully prepared when the time arrives. When the army has been arranged there seems to be no lack of courage to accept the gauntlet and fight soon commences, from that moment it is a game of chance and deceit for as no general plan of attack or combination of movements is ever previously arranged, the sole endeavour appears to be, to draw the opposite party into an ambush.

The General who directs, who is also the head warrior or chief, generally takes up his position well in rear, if possible near some large tree from whence is reported to him each change in the varying fortunes of the army. Some slight attempt at the subdivision of the force into divisions, Brigades or Regiments may be traced in their arrangements as also the keeping of Reserves, but the action resolves itself into a series of skirmishes. Their mode of fighting being altogether isolated and independent as regards each one individually. The movements of Brigades, Divisions in mass, hand to hand fighting, forcing of positions, and platoon firing being altogether unknown to them.

A native battle therefore may be assumed to be carried on invariably after the following plan; and here I may mention that during my stay in camp I have frequently discussed the subject with the head chiefs who took part in the Battle mentioned, and they all taught in the same school, though readily admitting the truth of the principles suggested, yet seemed extremely loath to depart from their usual habit.

The action commences with an order for each division: at the action at Ijaye there were four to send to the front; a tribe or portion which may be considered equivalent to a Regiment from a Brigade. They spread themselves out anyhow into open order, and skirmish away until their ammunition is exhausted upon which they retire to replenish.

Now herein consists one of the grand defects of their system. A having, we will suppose gained ground on his enemy B, the General never attempts to follow up and maintain his advantage by moving forward his reserve, but the whole army is kept at a standstill while the skirmish is going on in front.

When A retires therefore, to replenish his exhausted ammunition the front of the battle is left in exactly the same position that it was at the commencement, and there it would continue throughout the day, did not the enemy B usually at this period make an onward movement.

Now the deceitful element comes into play, and a feigned retreat is not unfrequently the result: this may or may not alter the fortunes of the day—if B advances in force, it is possible that a very hard tussle may take place, armed, however, with the musket, they avoid close quarters and form a habitual dislike to attacking walls, if A makes a stand B, in his turn will retire and once more the tide of battle rolls back to the original point. Occasionally if the ground is favourable, some attempt will be made to turn the flanks, but it as often results in failure.

Thus then proceeds the fight, a succession of advances and retreat, throughout the day until sunset, when, ammunition expended, begrimed and tired each side draws off, victory being claimed according to the returns of killed and wounded, which usually is not large—though thousands of rounds be fired, the killed may be counted by units and the wounded by tens. 17,000 men engaged in mortal combat on May 23rd, the killed on both sides, as ascertained by spies were 5 and the wounded under 50!

I can need scarcely add [sic] that having been on that occasion near enough to recognize the features of the enemy, I unhesitatingly declare, the feasibility of 1,000 well drilled soldiers under control being a match for ten times their number—for the advantages of discipline and system—we could add rifle practice versus the Long Dane, in many instances fired from the left side, held at the hip or held out at arm's length, and the intricate manœuvring of a Regt. to the irregular marching and skirmishing of a barbarous horde.

As at present commanded the Abbeokutan Army is gradually losing its prestige, so nobly won in action with Dahomey in 1851. The present commander is aged, the fire of his eye and elasticity of frame is gone, while enervated by luxurious ease, lowered by the claims of his numerous wives, the gross effeet old man passes his time in idleness and dissipation, instead of leading his dashing warriors to the fight.

During the action of May 23rd he never left his camp, and with such a commander the army is deserting in great numbers and a feeling of distrust has made serious inroads upon its efficiency. There are many young warriors in the Abbeokutan Army, however, and when placed in their hands, I believe it will be found a match for any neighbouring power.

That it would stand for a single hour against disciplined troops, is to belie one's senses, nor, in its present state of organization could much use, except as light troops to harass on the flanks, be made of this army in alliance with a disciplined force.

To sum up the result of my visit to the camp of Okemeji and Ijaye, the conversations with the generals, with most of whom I have established, I trust, a life long friendship, my own inspection of the men, their arms and mode of carrying on warfare according to native principles, and further taking into consideration that being now engaged for more than 15 months in a great war and against a powerful enemy, away from their own Towns, yet have been able under adverse circumstances, such as inefficient command, distance from supplies, denuding their own Towns of garrison, thereby rendering them liable to attack from any quarter, to hold their own: to have done all these leads me to the undoubted conclusion that the Army of Abbeokuta is capable of carrying on an offensive war against any native power with which it is liable to be brought in contact.

(Signed) A. Trefusis Jones,
Capt., 2nd W.I. Regt.

Abbeokuta
June 10th 1861.

MAPS AND PLANS

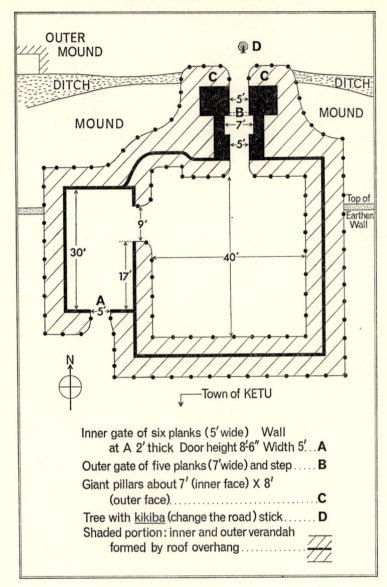

Inner gate of six planks (5′ wide)   Wall
    at A 2′ thick Door height 8′6″ Width 5′...**A**

Outer gate of five planks (7′wide) and step.....**B**

Giant pillars about 7′ (inner face) × 8′
    (outer face)...............................**C**

Tree with <u>kikiba</u> (change the road) stick.......**D**

Shaded portion: inner and outer verandah
    formed by roof overhang..............

1   Ground plan of Idena gate, Ketu, Dahomey

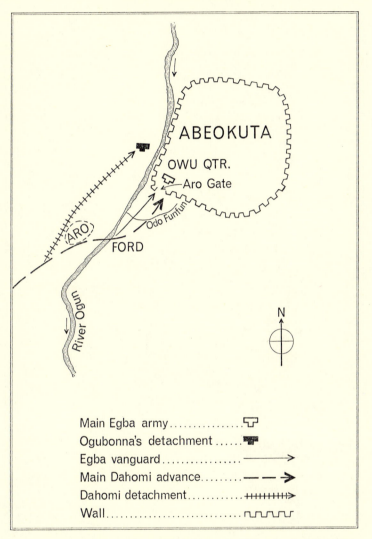

ABEOKUTA

OWU QTR.

Aro Gate

Odo Funfun

(ARO)

FORD

River Ogun

N

Main Egba army	⊓
Ogubonna's detachment	▓
Egba vanguard	⟶
Main Dahomi advance	— — ⟶
Dahomi detachment	+++++++⟶
Wall	⌐⌐⌐⌐⌐

4 Sketch to illustrate the battle of Abeokuta, 1851. The course of the wall in the sketch is based on a Colonial Office print of 1874 (reproduced in Biobaku). A Federal Survey plan of Abeokuta (1:12,500), 1930, shows more extensive defences, including a wall running north–south on the west bank of the river Ogun and opposite the town. These were probably built after 1857 as the Abeokuta continued to bear the brunt of the Dahomi attacks

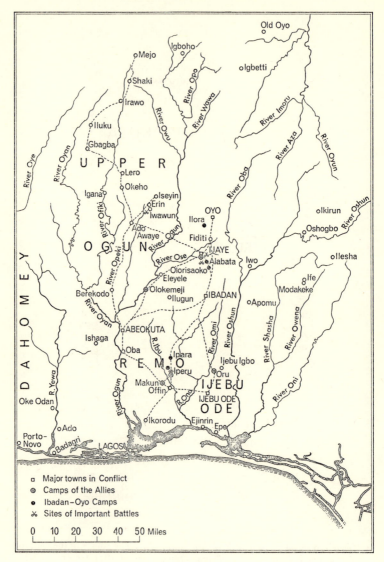

5   West and Central Yorubaland during the Ijaye War

to Imini

to Ilora
and Oyo

OJUTAYE

to
Iseyin

River Ose

IJAYE

A
C

B

AJEJA

Alore Watch
Post

BATTLEFIELD

River Ose

N

Site of
Egba Camp

to Eleyele and
Olokemeji

4000 feet

to Alabata,
Olorisaoko,
and Ibadan

∅ Present day Settlement
A Site of Kurunmi's Palace
B Site of Baptist Mission
C Probable site of Anglican Mission

6   Sketch of Ijaye in 1860–2

SELECT BIBLIOGRAPHY

I PRIMARY SOURCES

(a) *Government Papers*

(i) *Nigerian National Archives, Ibadan*

C.S.O. 8/1: Consular Letter Book, 1855–60.

C.S.O. 1/1: Despatches to Secretaries of State, 1861–5.

(ii) *Public Record Office, London*

FO84/1031, 1088, 1115, 1134, 1141, 1175, 1210, 1221: Consular Despatches, 1857–65.

FO84/1155: General Correspondence, 1861.

C.O. 267/270: Governor Hill's Despatches from Sierra Leone, 1861.

(iii) *Parliamentary Papers*

PP 1852 LIV (221): Papers Relative to the Reduction of Lagos.

PP 1860 LXIV (1): Slave Trade Correspondence, Africa (Consular).

PP 1862 LXI (339, 365): Papers Relating to the Occupation of Lagos.

PP 1863 XXXVIII (117): Papers Relating to the Destruction of Epe.

PP 1865 V (412): Report from the Select Committee on Africa (Western Coast).

(b) *Missionary Papers*

(i) *Church Missionary Society, London*

CA2/043: Letters and Journals of C. A. Gollmer.

CA2/045: Letters and Journals of Dr A. A. Harrison.

CA2/049: Letters and Journals of David Hinderer.

CA2/061: Letters and Journals of Thomas King.

CA2/064: Letters and Journals of J. A. Lamb.

CA2/066: Letters and Journals of Adolphus Mann.

CA2/068: Letters and Journals of S. A. Maser.

CA2/069: Letters and Journals of George Meakin.

CA2/085: Letters and Journals of Henry Townsend.

CA2/096: Letters and Diaries of J. B. Wood.

Iwe Irohin.

Church Missionary Intelligencer.

Church Missionary Proceedings.

Church Missionary Gleaner.

(ii) *Methodist Missionary Society, London*
The Correspondence of Edward Bickersteth, 1849–65.
Letters and Journals of Thomas Champness, 1860–3.
Letters of George Sharpe, 1863–5.
Letters of Christopher Sykes.
Wesleyan Methodist Missionary Notices.
Wesleyan Methodist Missionary Reports.

(iii) *Southern Baptist Convention, Richmond, Virginia, U.S.A.*
The Correspondence of A. D. Phillips, R. H. Stone and T. A. Reid.
The Commission.

(iv) *Société des Missions Africaines, Rome*
Journal of Rev. Father Broghero, 1863–4.
Les Missions Catholiques.

II SECONDARY SOURCES

(a) *Printed Sources*

AJISAFE, A. K. (alias E. O. Moore) (1924). *A History of Abeokuta.* London.

AKINYELE, I. B. (1948). *Iwe Itan Ibadan.* Ibadan.

BIOBAKU, S. O. (1957). *The Egba and their Neighbours, 1842–1872.* Oxford.

BOSMAN, W. (1907). *A New Accurate Description of the Coast of Guinea,* (1705). Facsimile edition, 1907.

BOWEN, T. J. (1857). *Adventures and Missionary Labours in several countries in the interior of Africa from 1849 to 1856.* Charleston.

BURNS, A. (1947). *A History of Nigeria.* London.

BURTON, R. F. (1863). *Abeokuta and the Camaroons Mountain.* London.

CHURCH MISSIONARY SOCIETY. *Register of Missionaries 1804–1894.*

CLAPPERTON, H. (1829). *Journal of a Second Expedition into the interior of Africa from the Bight of Benin to Soccattoo.* London.

CROWDER, MICHAEL (1962). *The Story of Nigeria.* London.

DIKE, K. O. (1956). *Trade and Politics in the Niger Delta 1830–1885.* Oxford.

DIKE, K. O. (ed.) (1960). *Eminent Nigerians of the Nineteenth Century.* Cambridge.

FAGE, J. D. (1959). *Introduction to the History of West Africa.* 2nd ed. Cambridge.

FORDE, D. (1951). *The Yoruba-Speaking Peoples of South-Western Nigeria.* London.

FREEMAN, T. B. (1844). *Journal of various visits to the interior of West Africa.* London.

FULLER, J. F. C. (1961). *The Conduct of War 1789–1961.* London.

GREENE, LIEUT.-COL. J. I. C. (ed.) (1945). *The Living Thoughts of Clausewitz.* London.

HERMAN-HODGE, H. B. (1929). *Gazetteer of Ilorin Province.* London.

HINDERER, ANNA (1872). *Seventeen Years in the Yoruba Country.* London.

HODGKIN, T. (1960). *Nigerian Perspectives.* Oxford.

JOHNSON, S. (1937). *The History of the Yorubas from the earliest times to the beginning of the British Protectorate.* C.M.S.

LANDER, R. and J. (1832). *Journal of an Expedition to explore the course and Termination of the Niger.* London.

LOSI, J. B. (1924). *History of Abeokuta.* Lagos.

NEWBURY, C. W. (1961). *The Western Slave Coast and its Rulers.* Oxford.

NIVEN, C. P. (1958). *A Short History of the Yoruba Peoples.* London.

OJO, CHIEF O. S. (n.d.) *Iwe Itan Saki.* Oyo.

OKUBOTE, M. BOTU (Apena). (1937). *Iwe Ikekuru ti Itan Ijebu.* Ibadan.

OLUGUNNA, D. (1959). *Osogbo.* Oshogbo.

OYERINDE, N. D. (1934). *Iwe Itan Ogbomoso.* Jos.

PALMER, H. R. (1928). *Sudanese Memoirs.* Lagos.

PARRINDER, E. G. (1956). *The Story of Ketu.* Ibadan.

STONE, R. H. (1900). *In Afric's Forest and Jungle or Six Years among the Yorubas.* Edinburgh.

THORP, ELLEN (1950). *The Swelling of Jordan.* London.

THORP, ELLEN (1956). *Ladder of Bones.* London.

TOY, SIDNEY (1955). *A History of Fortification.* London.

(b) *Articles*

BEIR, U. (1960). Oshogbo, Portrait of a Yoruba Town. *Nigeria Magazine*, October 1960.

BOAHEN, A. A. (1962). The Caravan Trade in the Nineteenth Century. *Journal of African History*, vol. III, no. 2.

DUNGLAS, E. (1949a). La première attaque des Dahoméenes contre Abeokuta. *Etudes Dahoméenes*, no. 1, 1949, I.F.A.N. A translated extract appeared in *Nigeria Magazine*, no. 64, March 1960.

DUNGLAS, E. (1949b). La deuxième attaque des Dahoméenes contre Abeokuta. *Etudes Dahoméenes*, no. 2, 1949, I.F.A.N.

LLOYD, P. C. (1954). The Traditional Political System of the Yoruba. *South-Western Journal of Anthropology*, vol. X, no. 4.

LLOYD, P. C. (1955). The Yoruba Lineage. *Africa*, vol. XXV, no. 3.

LLOYD, P. C. (1960). Sacred Kingship and Government among the Yoruba. *Africa*, vol. XXX.

MORTON-WILLIAMS, P. (1955). Some Yoruba kingdoms under modern conditions. *Journal of African Administration*, vol. VII, no. 4.

RYDER, A. F. C. (1961). The Benin Missions. *Journal of the Historical Society of Nigeria*, vol. II, no. 2.

SMITH, ROBERT S. (1962). Ijaiye, the Western Palatinate of the Yoruba. *Journal of the Historical Society of Nigeria*, vol. II, no. 3.

WILLETT, F. (1960). Investigations at Old Oyo, 1956–7, an Interim Report. *Journal of the Historical Society of Nigeria*, vol. II, no. 1.

(c) *Unpublished Works*

AJAYI, J. F. A. (1958). Christian Missions and the Making of Nigeria 1841–91. Ph.D. thesis, London.

CLARKE, W. H. Travels and Explorations 1854–8 (Nashville, Tenn. S.B.C. typescript.)

FADIPE, N. A. (1939). The Sociology of the Yoruba. Ph.D. thesis, London.

FREEMAN, T. B. (*c.* 1882). West Africa. MS. in the Methodist Archives, London. This MS. is dated 1882, though drafted earlier.

OMER-COOPER, J. D. (1960). A Preliminary Report on the History of Owu, an ancient Yoruba city. Paper presented before the Congress of the Historical Society of Nigeria.

INDEX

Abeokuta, Egba town, built (*c.* 1830), 11, 64; walls of, 24, 25, 27, 37; Egba centre, 15; communications with Lagos, 20, 93, 123, 128, with Ijaye, 108; attacked by Igebu (1832), 70; British guns given to (1851), 19, 90, 104, 131, 135; attacked by the Dahomi (1851), 9, 11, 32, 37–9, 50, 52, 71–2, 139; plan of battle, 145; threatened by Dahomi, 81, 93, 99, 108; British residents at, 81, 101; missionaries at, 60, 61, 70, 99n, 116n; Capt. Jones at, 104–5, 129, 132; refugees from Ijaye to (1861), 103, 110, 111; British vice-consul posted to (1862), 115, expelled, 116; attacked by the Dahomi (1864), 11, 55, 116–17; peace party at (1864), 118; Europe expelled from (1867), 121; *see also* Egba

Abiodun, Alafin of Oyo, 63, 64

Abogunrin, head slave and spokesman of Kurunmi, 106, 110

Accra, earthquake at, 116

Adamawa, Fulani at, 33

Adegunle Abeweila, Oni of Ife, 73

Adele I, Oba of Lagos, exiled to Badagry, 70

Adelu, Oyo crown prince, 76, 77; Alafin of Oyo, 77, 78, 79, 117

Ado, Egba camp at, 25; gate of, 27, 143; besieged by Egba (1840–53), 70, 72; British protectorate over, 115

Ado-Ekiti, Ewi of, 1

Afonja, Are-One-Kakanfo of Oyo, 11, 64

Agbabu, on Lagos lagoon, 121

Agbe Shango, capture of Osi Ilori of Ibadan at (1878), 46n

Agbodogun ('place where the mortars are heard'), 35

Ago-Oja, new Oyo capital at, 11, 29; *see also* Oyo, New

Agura, section of Egba, 69

Aisin (or Iba) river, 47

Ajase, 4; *see also* Porto Novo

Ajayi Ogboriefon, Balogun of Ibadan, 44, 45, 46–7, 81, 97; death, 49

Ajele, resident official, appointed by Ibadan at each place conquered, 44, 69

Ajibade, defeat of Egba and Ijaye at, 91

Ajisafe, A. K., 40n, 41n, 52n, 82n, 119n

Akati, Gaou of Dahomey, 37

Ake, section of Egba, 69; *see also* Alake of Ake

Akinjogbin, A. S., 11n

Akintola, Ibadan chief, son of Balogun Ibikunle, 46, 47

Akinyele, I. B., 69n, 113n

Akoko, Yoruba people, 2; invaded by Ibadan, 69, 122

Alabata, Ibadan camp at, 42, 91

Alafin of Oyo, 1, 2, 4; army of, 10, 13; conflict of Basorun with, 63, 124; Ibadan and, 73, 74, 122; *see also* Abiodun, Atiba, Majotu, Oluewu, Orompoto

Alake of Ake, 1, 15, 70, 99n, 115; Capt. Jones and, 129, 131, 132

Alaketu of Ketu, 1, 118

Alatayo, P., 48n

Ali, Hausa Balogun of Ilorin, 34, 35

Allada people, 10

Amazons of Dahomey army, 37, 39, 51n, 52

ammunition, manufacture of, 19, 40n, 134; supplies of, 19–21, 100, 112, 114, 128; given to Egba by British consul (1851), 38, 81; shortages of, 31, 40, 88, 108; exchange of slaves for, 125–6

Anago, language of Yoruba people, 2

Anoba, Are-Ona-Kakanfo of Egba, 42n; Balogun, 89, 90

Apata Ika, skirmish at, 76

Islam, 11, 60, 66, 77*n*
Iwawun, hilltop town, 23; captured by Ibadan (1860), 42, 97
Iwe Irohin, 82*n*, 84*n*
Iwo, refugees in, 64
Iyalode, head of women chiefs, 39, 87; *see also* Tinubu

Jalumi ('rush into the water') war (1878), 18*n*, 47
Jenne, trade of Oyo with, 3
jihad of Fulani, 23, 33, 34, 55, 64
Johnson, H., catechist, 81
Johnson, S., historian of Oyo, 9, 10*n*, 11*n*, 13, 14, 21*n*, 25, 27*n*, 29, 30, 33, 34*n*, 35, 37, 40, 41*n*, 42*n*, 44, 48, 51, 52*n*, 61, 69*n*, 73*n*, 75*n*, 76*n*, 80*n*, 82*n*, 86*n*, 87*n*, 89*n*, 90*n*, 92*n*, 93*n*, 97*n*, 98, 102*n*, 103*n*, 105*n*, 108*n*, 110*n*, 111*n*, 114*n*, 117*n*, 118*n*, 119*n*
Jones, Capt. A. T., West India Regiment, on Abeokuta and Egba army (1861), vi, 10, 14, 15, 16, 18, 19, 21, 22, 25, 26, 27*n*, 28, 30–1, 40, 41, 50, 54, 104–5, 129–40; death of, 105

Kano, trade of Oyo with, 3; muskets on sale at (1851), 17*n*
Kehere, Balogun of Ipara, 92
Ketu, Yoruba people, Alaketu of, 1, 118; conquered by Oyo, 4; walls and gates of, 24, 26, 27, 142; Dahomi in, 37, 52; conquered by Dahomi, 2, 12; occupied by the French (1890's), 12
King, T., 90*n*, 91*n*
Kiriji, Ekiti war round, 12, 21, 122
Kishi, double wall of, 24
Koso, sacred grove near Ijaye, 88
Koso, walls of, 25
Kosoko, exiled king of Lagos, 20
Kurunmi of Ijaye, given title of Are-Ona-Kakanfo by Alafin Atiba, 29, 67; in Ijaye war, 40, 61, 88–90, 97–9; death of, 42, 105–6; death of sons of, 42, 97
Kutuje war, Ibadan name for last (or Iperu) phase of Ijaye war, 113–22

Lagos, Yoruba town, 13*n*; annexed by British, 12, 106; exiled rulers of,

20, 70; slave market of, 51; trade and traders of, 12*n*, 100, 115; Ibadan communications with, 128; and Ikorodu market, 20, 119, 120; British administration at, 60, 109, 116; British expansion from, 120, 121; Madam Tinubu expelled from, 128*n*; arms and ammunition from, 20, 126, 128
Lamb, Rev. A., 115
Lander, J. and Lander, R., travellers, 9, 23*n*, 24, 26, 53
Latosisa, Are of Ibadan, 45, 95, 97
Lekki, annexed by British, 115
Lodder, Lt, R.N., 84
Long Dane flintlock muskets, 18, 20, 134, 139
Losi, J. B., 89*n*

McCoskry, W., British consul at Lagos, 12*n*, 21, 104*n*, 105, 123, 129
Mai Idris Alooma, ruler of Bornu, 17
Majotu, Alafin of Oyo, 9*n*
Makun, Ijebu-Remo town, besieged by Ijaye and Egba, 112, 117; Egba withdraw to, at truce, 118; raided by Ikorodu, 119; visited by Madam Tinubu, 128*n*
Mann, Rev. A., Anglican missionary, 42, 51, 74*n*, 79*n*, 89*n*, 95*n*, 99*n*, 103*n*, 108*n*, 109–10
Maser, S. A., C.M.S. missionary, 94*n*
Maxim guns, 12
Meakin, G., 75*n*, 77*n*, 78*n*, 79*n*, 81*n*
missionaries, and Yoruba language, 2; and sources of Ijaye War, 60–1; and supply of arms to Abeokuta, 19, 20, protest at selling of captives, 99*n*; and famine in Ijaye town, 94, 98, 103
Modakeke, near Ile-Ife, 64, 73
Mugba-Mugba ('locust-fruit') war, 15
Mulliner, acting-governor of Lagos, 115
muskets, 17, 18, 31, 84, 88

naval squadron (anti-slavery), 81, 100, 104, 120
Newbury, C. W., 20, 101*n*, 115*n*, 124*n*, 126
Nigeria, British protectorate over, 12

night-fighting, at Oshogbo, 35–6, 43

Nupe, struggle with Oyo, 3, 4; muskets imported via, 17n; in Ijaye war, 59; as mercenaries, 81, 85

Oba of Benin, 1

Oba river, 45

Obas, Yoruba, 5, 65

Odenlo (Oderinlo), Balogun of Ibadan army at Oshogbo, 34, 35

Oduduwa, mythical ancestor, 1, 2

Offa, advance of Ibadan towards (1840's), 69; and battle of Ikirun (1878), 47, 48, 49

Ofin, gate of, 27

Ogbomosho, refugees in, 64; Baptist agent at, 85n

Ogboni (Oboni), civil leaders of Yoruba, 71, of Egba, 83, 99n, 132, 133

Ogboni staff of Ibadan chiefs, symbol of authority, 79

Ogedengbe, leader of Ekiti against Ibadan, 122

Ogun river, Old Oyo territory on both sides of, 4, 63; crossings of, in connection with Dahomi attacks on Abeokuta, 37, 38, 116–17; Egba camp by (1860), 41; slaughter by the Dahomi of Egba farmers along, 39, 51

Ogun, Upper, district, conquered by Ijaye, 67; Ibadan dispute Ijaye claim to, 78, 93–5, 97, 102, 125; Ibadan obtain hold on, 42, 111; inherited by Oyo, 122

Ogunbona, Egba chief, 38, 39, 41, 93, 130

Ogunmola, Otun Balogun of Ibadan, 40, 42, 43, 50n, 51, 80, 82, 86, 96, 97, 98, 102, 106, 108, 112, 113, 114, 117; Ilori, son of, 44, 45

Oheko, Oyo-Ijaye affray at, 78

Oja, founder of Ago-Oja, later New Oyo, 76; Ashipa, descendant of, 77

Oje, Ijaye chief, 94

Ojo, O. S., 34n

Oke Kere, fortified hill near Ipara, 113

Oke Odan, 72, 99; British protectorate over, 115

Oke Ogun (Upper Ogun), see Ogun, Upper

Oke Ona, section of Egba, 69

Okeigbo, route from Lagos inland through, 122

Okubote, M. B., 112n, 113n

Okukenu, Ogboni chief, later Alake of Ake, 70

Okuku, village, 47, 48

Old Oyo, see Oyo, Old

Ologun, military leaders of Egba, 71, 87n

Olokemeji, Egba base at, 41, 93, 129, 130, 136

Olokuku of Okuku, 47n

Olorisaoko, Ibadan camp at, 86, 90, 102, 108; battle at, 98

Olowu of Owu, 1

Oluewu, Alafin of Oyo, 14n, 76

Olugunna, D., 34n

Oluyole of Ibadan, appointed Basorun by Alafin Atiba, 29, 68, 82n

Omer-Cooper, J. D., 25n

Ondo, Yoruba people, 2; Oyo and, 4, 63; route from Lagos inland through, 122

Oni of Ife, 73, 118

Onisabe of Sabe, 1

Oparinu, Arin Oje of Inisha, 48n

Oranyan, mythical founder of Old Oyo, youngest son of Oduduwa, 2; sacrifice to, 80

Ore of Ottun, 1

Orisas, deities, originated at Ile-Ife, 1

Orompoto, Alafin of Oyo, 3

Oru, Ijebu base, 93

Ose river, 41, 108; battles of, 87–8, 94

Osemawe of Ondo, 1

Oshogbo, walls of, 24, 34; defeat of Fulani at (c. 1840), 11, 16, 18, 23, 32, 33–6, 43, 55

Oshun river, 34, 45n; goddess of, 36

Osi, title of commander of left wing in battle, 14, 79; see also Ilori of Ibadan

Otin river, 47; goddess of, 48

Otta, conquered by Egba, 70

Ottun, besieged by Ilorin, 73

Otun, title of commander of right wing in battle, 14

Otun Balogun, see Ogunmola